# GUITAR GODS

**Publisher and Creative Director:** Nick Wells
**Project Editor and Picture Research:** Sara Robson
**Art Director and Layout Design:** Mike Spender
**Digital Design and Production:** Chris Herbert

**Special thanks to:** Jason Draper, Rebecca Kidd, Victoria Lyle, Chris McNab, Geoffrey Meadon,
Sonya Newland, Polly Prior and Catherine Taylor

Metro Books
122 Fifth Avenue
New York, NY10011

ISBN: 978-1-4351-2073-0

Printed and bound in China

1 3 5 7 9 10 8 6 4 2

# GUITAR GODS

RUSTY CUTCHIN, HUGH FIELDER, MIKE GENT, MICHAEL MUELLER, DAVE SIMONS

CONSULTANT EDITOR: RUSTY CUTCHIN
FOREWORD BY MICK TAYLOR

METRO BOOKS
NEW YORK

# CONTENTS

4

6

9

# FOREWORD

My life changed forever the first time I heard Stevie Ray Vaughan wrestle a fistful of mesmerizing notes from his Fender Stratocaster. Exactly why it should have been him, at that point in time, who ignited a pre-teenager's flame for the instrument isn't clear, but ask any guitar player and they'll tell you a broadly similar story. It will be a definable moment, brought into razor-sharp focus by an unforgettable aural and visual experience. Something 'speaks' to you profoundly; something makes a connection so powerful that life thereafter seems unthinkable without this strange amalgam of metal, plastic and wood. Moreover, without hearing that strange amalgam in the hands of a master.

Masters is what this book is all about – from Duane Allman to Frank Zappa these are players who have famously, infamously perhaps, built and cemented the six-stringers' iconic status in the twentieth and twenty-first centuries. As the perfect example, take former Guns N' Roses guitar slinger Slash. The long hair flows in the wind, cigarette planted permanently on his bottom lip. Posturing bare-chested in a desert, he throws his Gibson Les Paul forward, leans back and launches into a huge, searing solo. It's Slash against the world – his guitar is his attack, his defence and his voice. For many young guitar enthusiasts as the Nineties dawned, that was the moment that their lives changed forever, the moment the connection was made.

Over a half-century earlier came a young man named Aaron Thibeaux 'T-Bone' Walker. Long before Yngwie Malmsteen and Jimi Hendrix, here was a guy playing the guitar behind his back or between his legs while simultaneously earning a reputation as one of the very first electric guitarists to play melodic, single-note lines (solos to you and me). Just imagine if you'd been a teenager back then – a teenager like Riley B. King, better known of course as B.B. Floored by T-Bone's sound and style, the young B.B. was compelled to go out and buy an electric guitar. Before you know it, we're into a gargantuan pyramid selling-style network of influence; thousands of people across the world transfixed by the magnificent noise and mesmerizing image of this almost laughably simple instrument being abused. Chuck Berry duckwalked, Hendrix played with his teeth and behind his head, and Pete

Townshend threw his through his amplifiers. They came from radically different backgrounds, played wildly different styles, but what they shared – what is shared by today's heroes – is an undeniable rebel status. The guitar is rock'n'roll, regardless of whether it's being played by Satriani or Segovia.

Quite why it has worked out like that is for the psychologists to debate. Many have pointed to the obvious sexual allure of the lead guitar performance, others have suggested that it attracts a certain kind of character: egocentric, cocky, adversarial. It doesn't take too much brainwork to think of any number of examples, which if you'll forgive me, prompts one of my favourite jokes of all time... How many guitarists does it take to change a light bulb? 100 – one to change the light bulb and the other 99 to say they could have done it better.

Of course, being a guitar god is about much more than throwing shapes or, ahem, Strats. There's the small matter of what you play. Think about Jimmy Page's opening phrase to 'Whole Lotta Love', Eric Clapton's blistering theme in 'Layla' or Jack White's fuzzy riff in 'Seven Nation Army'. These sounds will move people forever – once again, guitar and guitarist versus the world.

Whatever the reasons, however we got here, every one of the gods in this A–Z is identifiable by a mere handful of notes or inflections in their playing, a remarkable fact when you consider that the guitar itself has remained unchanged in any fundamental sense since the mid–Fifties. More than any other instrument, the guitar simultaneously demands and delivers individuality on the part of the player. It enables unsurpassed freedom of expression that contributes to a constantly evolving melting pot of ideas and influences that continue to shape everything we know about music. These swaggering six–stringers have been central in the soundtrack to life and popular culture as we know it. Sometimes it's merely a case of right place, right time. In other cases it's been a relentless pursuit of discovery and betterment. So dare we deify the much–lauded pickers and strummers? Should we worship at the alter of six strings?

Of course we should.

**Mick Taylor**

# INTRODUCTION

On an internet guitar forum a participant once inquired about a certain model of guitar, the instrument supposedly descended from the Egyptian lyre, which according to legend was created by Tehuti, the god of wisdom, whom the Greeks called Hermes or Pan. The online enthusiast was seeking information on the defunct guitar brand Eros, named after one of the four expressions of love in Greek mythology: eros, storge, philia and agape (romantic, familial, brotherly and charitable or god-like). One practical reader responded, 'I have no info on it, but plug that s*** in and see how it sounds!'

Passion, power, tradition, history – can all these qualities be assigned to any other musical instrument in the twenty–first century? And can any other instrument endowed with such mythological qualities play the dual role of lover and enemy? To be caressed one moment in tenderness by the acolytes of B.B. King and Eric Clapton and destroyed in rage the next by the disciples of Pete Townshend and Kurt Cobain?

The gods clearly answered 'yes' to the multifaceted role guitar played throughout its development in the twentieth century, and the children of the gods – of those earthbound deities described in the following pages – have responded with praise, adulation and worship, as well as a devotion to becoming god–like themselves, making guitar far and away the most popular musical instrument in the world.

But how does a guitarist attain powers and abilities far beyond those of mortal musicians? Guitar gods come from all races and nationalities. They share a dedication to art, an intense respect for craft, a willingness to sacrifice and suffer for their sound. They sweat and toil until, like Heracles, they reach immortality, rising to musical Olympus on the strength of their many labours – attaining virtuosity in playing, recording and stagecraft. (Heracles, after all, killed his music teacher Linus with a lyre, inspiring the idea of the guitar as a tool for any occasion.)

But it all means nothing if it doesn't sound good when you plug that s*** in. Though the original guitar heroes (and several descendants) played acoustically, it was the fire of electricity that paved the way to the pantheon for mortal guitarists. Developing a unique sound – a tone! – with pickups, amplifiers and speakers, became crucial to building the legacy and legend of the guitar gods you're about to discover or revisit. As each player took his or her place on the mountain, followers throughout the world recognized and paid tribute to the talent and dedication of these icons regardless of genre. The guitarists herein may not be the only great musicians, but they are the leaders who have revolutionized the way we listen, respond and live our lives to music.

The gods that we have chosen to honour in this book possess heroic qualities of one sort or another: virtuosity, a pioneering spirit, raw power, courage to forge new paths, dedication and passion for what they do. They come from different backgrounds and have different musical heritages, but the one quality they all share is a sheer, mind-blowing talent. Let's take a look at how we selected them.

The virtuosi are the iconic names of rock'n'roll (Jimmy Page, Jeff Beck, Eddie Van Halen and Jimi Hendrix, to name a few); these are the guitarists whose lives are about the playing – the talent, the technique and, above all, the dedication. The dedication of practising for hours every day, cultivating the talent and the technique, obsessing over sounds and how to create and control them and then putting it all into a performance onstage. The guitar hero inspires the audience, but the guitar virtuoso also inspires and influences other guitarists, who can see beyond the image to the dedication and details in the music and the performance.

In musicians such as Robert Johnson, John Lee Hooker and Albert King we celebrate the pioneering spirit, those who channelled the hard times of the American south, and the inheritors (Buddy Guy, Stevie Ray Vaughan), who helped the blues continue to be a driving force as rock'n'roll matured into rock music. American rhythm and blues influenced legends such as The Rolling Stones and The Animals, and evolved into hard rock and heavy metal, beginning with the bone-rattling blues of Led Zeppelin and others. The sound of the blues and its messengers also evolved from the solo singer–guitarist to the electrified wailer fronting a band – but the primal 12–bar structure and the raw emotion of the singers and players remained the bedrock of the blues.

In the Fifties the pioneering spirit was still strong. The likes of Chuck Berry, Bo Diddley and Scotty Moore were the founding fathers of rock'n'roll, the product of black music combined with white, of blues mixed with country. Their music influenced the next generation, and as the Sixties progressed styles began to change as pop toughened into rock. For some guitarists in this category the blues was a jumping-off point from which to develop different approaches such as psychedelia, progressive rock and hard rock. Others preferred to stay closer to the original spirit of the blues. Meanwhile, the role of lead guitarist was elevated to even greater heights; the era of the guitar god had truly arrived.

What qualities does the heavy metal guitarist display? Jazz has its saxophonists. Blues has its harmonica players. Pop has its synthesizers and dancers. But take the guitar hero out of hard rock and heavy metal, and you've gutted

the genre. Nowhere has the guitar had a greater impact than on the sound and style of heavy music, and no other genre of music has produced as many guitar gods. In Tony Iommi's spine-chilling tritones and John 5's twisted, high-tech fretboard fury, the dark power of the heavy metal guitar god is truly unleashed.

Some guitar heroes blaze trails with fiery histrionics and outrageous behaviour while others simply revolutionize music with good taste and a unique sound. There can be no doubt that the 12-string shimmer of Roger McGuinn, the inspiring textures of The Edge and the history-making lead lines of George Harrison made these legendary icons burn as brightly as their hard-rock counterparts. They passed the torch to a new generation that would pour fuel onto the rock'n'roll fire, even as direct descendants such as Trey Anastasio and Lenny Kravitz continued to create new and tasty licks in both high- and low-intensity musical settings.

Becoming a virtuoso requires heroic effort, but not all guitar heroes choose the life of the rock star. As befits rock's heritage in the marriage of country and rhythm and blues, many of music's greatest guitarists choose country or jazz as the genre for their life's work. Rock players are inspired by the great guitarists of bluegrass, classical, flamenco, fusion and other disciplines, and today many players of those styles, in turn, start out 'in the woodshed', learning Clapton, Page and Beck to help master the guitar skills that exist in the world beyond rock.

And then there are those musicians of a certain mindset, who would probably regard the term 'guitar god' with suspicion. They are the indie and alternative rock guitarists. Although its roots lie in late-Seventies punk, indie and alternative rock have broadened to embrace such a diversity of guitar styles as to render labels irrelevant, particularly when many acts have crossed over into the mainstream and sold millions of records. For the majority of these musicians, the guitar is a tool that serves the song; the effect achieved by the music, not the technical skill of the player, is of paramount importance.

As the ancient gods did battle with nature, mortals and each other, these modern-day gods have battled the winds of change and the mortal taste for the next big sound, sometimes losing their place on the mountain or climbing to the top again after odysseys filled with failure and self-examination. But these artists have inspired millions with their passion, their drive and their determination to devote their lives to music.

From the players whose flame died too early to the veterans whose fires burned well into their 90s, each unique guitarist left something – a solo, a song, an album – that has challenged a young guitarist to climb the mountain as well. The stories of their lives are often as compelling as their recorded works, and the names alone – Hendrix, Van Halen, Page, Beck, Clapton (the first publicly acknowledged guitar god) – evoke passions as intense as the ones stirred by their music.

But it is the music that matters most, and gods must not only be studied – they must be heard. The soaring solos, the rich textures, the rhythmic chop, the angry power chord – these are the calling cards of the great guitarists. The bite of a Telecaster, the quiet roar of a humbucker, the relaxing gurgle of a phase shifter, the glorious warmth of a vacuum tube in an amplifier – these are the tools that, in the hands of the people in this book, transformed mere musicians into immortals. Plug them in and see how they sound.

# DUANE ALLMAN

## SOUTHERN SLIDE STAR

At first a country duo, Duane Allman and his brother Gregg were converted to the blues when they saw B.B. King performing. They began playing professionally in 1961, first in the Allman Joys and then the Hour Glass, which split in early 1968. Around this time Allman began playing electric slide, using an empty glass medicine bottle.

The Hour Glass recording led to session work on Wilson Pickett's *Hey Jude* (1968) album, which in turn led to a place as a full-time session musician at Muscle Shoals Studio in Alabama. Frustration at the limitations of session playing led Allman to form The Allman Brothers Band in March 1969 with Gregg (organ, vocals), Dickey Betts (second lead), Berry Oakley (bass) and drummers Butch Trucks and Jai Johanny 'Jaimoe' Johanson. They made their recorded debut on *The Allman Brothers Band* (1969), and built momentum with *Idlewild South* (1970). In 1971 they recorded the seminal *At Fillmore East*, which captured their incendiary double-lead guitar attack at its peak. Allman was killed in a motorcycle accident a few months later. Admired not only for his slide technique, Allman was also much esteemed for the improvisatory skills he displayed on his 1959 Gibson Darkburst Les Paul and 1968 Gibson Cherry SG.

### DATE OF BIRTH/DEATH

20 November 1946/29 October 1971

### PLACE OF BIRTH

Nashville, USA

### GENRES

Southern Rock, Blues Rock, Blues, Jazz Fusion, Jam

# TREY ANASTASIO

## STAR OF THE JAM SCENE

Trey Anastasio became the star of the jam-band resurgence through his prolific work both with his band Phish and a multitude of side projects. Inheriting the mantle and rabid following of The Grateful Dead and its departed guitar hero Jerry Garcia, Anastasio displayed a deep knowledge of rock, blues, jazz and country guitar styles. He formed Phish at university with bassist Mike Gordon, drummer Jon Fishman and guitarist Jeff Holdsworth (later replaced by keyboardist Page McConnell). The group developed its loyal following by combining progressive rock-influenced compositions with a genial, inventive stage show. Constant touring helped the band's sound develop into highly focused works such as *Rift* (1993) and on to more fundamentally improvisational works, including *The Story Of The Ghost* (1997) and *The Siket Disc* (1998).

Anastasio has always played hollow-body electrics built by his friend and former audio technician Paul Languedoc. Since the dissolution of Phish, he has appeared onstage with many artists, including Phil Lesh & Friends, reaffirming Anastasio's allegiance to the legacy of The Grateful Dead. He ran afoul of the law as a result of drug use in 2007, and was sidelined for part of 2008. In 2009 he made a triumphant return to the stage, playing with Phish and leading the New York Philharmonic on 12 September at Carnegie Hall.

**DATE OF BIRTH**

30 September 1964

**PLACE OF BIRTH**

Fort Worth, USA

**GENRES**

Jam, Rock, Progressive Rock, Jazz Fusion

A-Z OF
GUITAR GODS

# CHET ATKINS

## MR GUITAR

The first superstar instrumentalist to emerge from the modern Nashville recording scene, with a legendary right-hand finger-picking style, Chet Atkins was also a producer, engineer, label executive and Artists & Repertoire (A&R) man without peer. He began his career touring with regional South and Midwest stars, before being signed by RCA in 1947. His early recordings didn't sell, however, and it wasn't until 1954 that he had his first hit single, 'Mr Sandman'. He also became a design consultant for Gretsch, who manufactured a popular Chet Atkins line of electric guitars.

In 1957, Atkins was put in charge of RCA's Nashville division. With country music record sales slumping in the wake of rock'n'roll, Atkins helped create the pop-crossover genre that became known as the Nashville Sound. By 1968 he was vice-president of RCA's country division, having brought the likes of Waylon Jennings, Willie Nelson and Dolly Parton to the label. Atkins left RCA in the Seventies. He signed with Columbia and released his first album for them in 1983. He also began designing guitars for Gibson. In the Nineties he continued to release albums, including duo projects with Suzy Bogguss and Mark Knopfler. Atkins died of colon cancer in June 2001. He was inducted into the Rock And Roll Hall Of Fame the following year.

### DATE OF BIRTH/DEATH

20 June 1924/30 June 2001

### PLACE OF BIRTH

Luttrell, USA

### GENRES

Country, Pop Crossover

# SYD BARRETT

## FLOYD'S DESTRUCTIVE GENIUS

Legendary 'lost' psychedelic genius Syd Barrett joined the embryonic Pink Floyd while attending art college in London, and they soon developed the improvisational style that made them the premier band of the city's underground scene. In January 1967, their debut single 'Arnold Layne' was a minor hit and was followed by the Top 10 success 'See Emily Play'. Barrett penned both, although neither was truly representative of the band in concert. Barrett's short whimsical songs also dominate *Piper At The Gates Of Dawn* (1967). By the time of its release, however, Barrett's behaviour had become increasingly unpredictable, and his LSD–induced breakdown saw him permanently replaced by David Gilmour in 1968.

Barrett's solo career was short, consisting of *The Madcap Laughs* and *Barrett* (both 1970), and *Opel* (1988), a collection of outtakes and unreleased material. After some ill–fated live outings as a member of Stars in 1972 and an abortive return to the studio in 1974, Barrett retreated to Cambridge, where his reclusive lifestyle fuelled the legend. An innovative guitarist, Barrett achieved unique effects by playing through a Binson echo unit and employing a Zippo lighter or plastic ruler as bottlenecks. His favoured instrument was a Telecaster Esquire decorated with mirrors.

### DATE OF BIRTH/DEATH

6 January 1946/7 July 2006

### PLACE OF BIRTH

Cambridge, England

### GENRES

Rock, Blues, R&B, Psychedelia

A-Z OF
GUITAR GODS

# JEFF BECK
## YARDBIRDS TO PIONEER

Mercurial genius Jeff Beck found fame with The Yardbirds in 1965, where his vibrant, fearless playing was a major element of hits such as 'Heart Full Of Soul'. He abruptly quit the band in 1966 and after the solo hit 'Hi Ho Silver Lining' he spent time first with the Jeff Beck Group and then Beck, Bogert & Appice. The latter's funk–rock sound was evident on both *Rough And Ready* (1972) and *Beck, Bogert & Appice* (1973), but the group lacked a singer to match the instrumental pyrotechnics, and by 1974 Beck was on his own again.

The solo, all–instrumental, funk–infused *Blow By Blow* (1975) was Beck's most successful album and the follow–up, *Wired* (1976), took the jazz–rock fusion a stage further. His later albums continued to take bold and diverse directions. *Flash* (1985) confronted the Eighties style of rock guitar as well as disco. Techno beats and electronica provided the backdrop for *You Had It Coming* (2001) and *Jeff* (2003). *Live Beck!*, recorded in 2003, and *Live Bootleg USA 06* (both 2006) finally did justice to his concert performances. Beck's preferred guitar is a Fender Telecaster. He gets his distinctive sound by using his fingers rather than a plectrum and using the tremolo arm and a wah–wah pedal. Inducted into the Rock And Roll Hall Of Fame, his new album, *Emotion & Commotion*, was released in April 2010.

**DATE OF BIRTH**

24 June 1944

**PLACE OF BIRTH**

Wallington, England

**GENRES**

Rock, Funk Rock, Jazz Rock, Blues Rock, Heavy Metal, Jazz Fusion, Electronica

A–Z OF
GUITAR GODS

# ADRIAN BELEW

## AN UNDERRATED SIX-STRINGER

Best known for his Eighties stint in King Crimson, underrated six-stringer Adrian Belew is able to make his Parker Deluxe guitar not only sing but also scream, squawk, roar, tweet and talk in elephant tongue. He joined popular Nashville-area cover band Sweetheart in 1975, and two years later Frank Zappa caught a show and recruited Belew to join his own band. Later Belew accompanied David Bowie on his 1978 world tour and appears on the albums *Stage* (1978) and *Lodger* (1979).

Belew met Talking Heads producer Jerry Harrison, who invited him to contribute to their 1980 album *Remain In Light* and then continue on as a touring guitarist. On the tour Belew met guitarist Robert Fripp, who invited him to join a reconstructed King Crimson. Abandoning their prog-rock roots for a more modern, Talking Heads-style sound, Crimson recorded three acclaimed albums – *Discipline* (1981), *Beat* (1982) and *Three Of A Perfect Pair* (1984) – before disbanding. Belew spent the next few years recording solo, as a member of the Bears and as a session guitarist. In 1995 he reunited with his Crimson mates to record *THRAK*, and has since recorded two more King Crimson albums. Currently, Belew explores new musical frontiers in his Power Trio.

**DATE OF BIRTH**

23 December 1949

**PLACE OF BIRTH**

Covington, USA

**GENRES**

Progressive Rock, New Wave, Funk Rock

# MATTHEW BELLAMY

## RULER OF THE RIFF

Twenty-first century guitar god Matthew Bellamy first took up piano lessons as a boy before turning to the guitar, equally inspired by Ray Charles and classical music. In the mid-Nineties, Bellamy formed Muse with Chris Wolstenholme (bass) and Dominic Howard (drums). The band served their apprenticeship through constant gigging while soaking up more influences, notably Jeff Buckley and Radiohead. After an independently released EP, Muse signed a major deal in 1998. Debut album *Showbiz* (1999) marked them as a band with potential crossover appeal to fans of indie, metal and prog rock. *Origin Of Symmetry* (2001) was a more expansive collection, and Bellamy's riff from 'Plug In Baby' has been hailed as one of the greatest of all time. *Absolution* (2003) developed the classical influences, and Bellamy's lyrical themes of Armageddon, conspiracy and corruption were further explored on *Black Holes And Revelations* (2006). Bellamy and Muse took control of production for *The Resistance* (2009), which built upon Bellamy's classical infatuation.

Bellamy uses guitars made by Manson of Exeter, principally a silver model that he helped design. Among its customized features is a built-in fuzzbox, through which he achieves his unique sound. He has also played a Fender Stratocaster, a Gibson SG, a Les Paul and a Yamaha Pacifica.

### DATE OF BIRTH

9 June 1978

### PLACE OF BIRTH

Cambridge, England

### GENRES

Rock, Alternative Rock, Progressive Rock, Classical

# GEORGE BENSON
## SMOOTH JAZZ SUPERSTAR

George Benson started out playing straight–ahead instrumental jazz with organist Jack McDuff. At 21, Benson recorded his first album as leader, *The New Boss Guitar* (1964), with McDuff on organ. Benson's next recording was *It's Uptown With The George Benson Quartet* (1965), which showcased Benson's talent in constructing swinging bebop lines at blistering tempos. He recorded with Miles Davis in the mid–Sixties and attempted to follow in his idol Wes Montgomery's footsteps by recording jazz versions of pop albums such as The Beatles' *Abbey Road* (1969) and *White Rabbit* (1972). In 1975 he signed with Warner Brothers – and then came *Breezin'* (1976). 'This Masquerade' – the first single to top the pop, R&B and jazz charts simultaneously – made Benson a star. He followed up with the hits 'On Broadway', 'Give Me The Night', 'Turn Your Love Around' and others. Benson accumulated three other platinum LPs and two gold albums at Warner. Since then he has travelled the world and recorded and performed with orchestras and a host of music stars.

Throughout his career Benson infused his records with cool-jazz virtuoso guitar solos, played at first on a Gibson L5 and later on one of the Signature GB10 or GB200 models developed for him by Ibanez.

**DATE OF BIRTH**

22 March 1943

**PLACE OF BIRTH**

Pittsburgh, USA

**GENRES**

Jazz, Pop, R&B, Soul

A-Z OF
GUITAR GODS

# CHUCK BERRY

## ROCK'N'ROLL'S PIONEER

Despite several stints in prison, the rock'n'roll pioneer's career flourished from the Fifties to the Seventies. Berry began playing blues mixed with ballads and hillbilly with The Johnnie Johnson Trio, but a signing with the Chess label resulted in a change of direction. 'Maybellene' (1955) was one of the first rock'n'roll singles and became a Top 5 hit in America. The string of hits that followed, including the seminal 'Johnny B. Goode', set the template for rock'n'roll for many years to come. His hits of the Sixties included standards such as 'No Particular Place To Go' and 'You Never Can Tell'.

Berry's only No. 1 single was the suggestive novelty ditty 'My Ding-a-Ling' (1970), which reached the top of the charts in both the US and the UK. For the rest of the Seventies, Berry toured extensively. He travelled alone, hiring a local band to back him at each performance, confident that they would be familiar with his material. This has led to accusations that his gigs as slapdash and out of tune, although Berry has been known to sometimes deliberately detune his guitar for effect. He made his last studio album in 1979, but has continued to perform, including a European tour in 2008.

### DATE OF BIRTH

18 October 1926

### PLACE OF BIRTH

St Louis, USA

### GENRES

Rock'n'Roll, Blues

# NUNO BETTENCOURT

## EXTREME GUITAR STAR

Born in the Portuguese archipelago of the Azores, guitarist and songwriter Bettencourt grew up in Boston, Massachusetts. He joined Extreme in 1985, and the band released its self-titled debut album in 1989. In 1991 came *Pornograffitti*, which included the acoustic hits 'More Than Words' and 'Hole Hearted'. But it was the extraordinary technical prowess Bettencourt displayed on tunes such as 'Get The Funk Out' and 'He-Man Woman Hater' that solidified his reputation as one of the era's top guitarists. It was also during this time that Washburn guitars unveiled the Nuno Bettencourt N4 signature-model guitar.

After Extreme disbanded in 1996, Bettencourt released his solo debut, *Schizophonic* (1997), on which he played all instruments. His next group, Mourning Widows, incorporated a variety of alternative-rock styles. Their self-titled debut in 1998 was followed by *Furnished Souls For Rent*, released in Japan in 2000. In 2002, Bettencourt formed the recording entity Population 1 and released *Population 1. Sessions From Room 4* followed in 2004. The band changed its name to the DramaGods and released *Love* in 2005. In 2007, Bettencourt teamed up with singer Perry Farrell in Satellite Party, releasing *Ultra Payloaded* that same year, but Bettencourt departed soon after its release and has recently played live with pop/R&B star Rihanna.

### DATE OF BIRTH

20 September 1966

### PLACE OF BIRTH

Praia da Vitória, Portugal

### GENRES

Pop, Rock, Alternative Rock

# DICKEY BETTS

## THE 'GOLDIE' TOUCH

Southern blues–rock guitarist Dickey Betts was leading a group called The Second Coming when he met the other members of what became The Allman Brothers Band. His role as second lead guitarist, with Duane Allman, gave the band its trademark dual–lead sound, captured most potently on *At Fillmore East* (1971). Betts became sole lead guitarist on Allman's death later that year, and wrote several of their most celebrated songs, including 'In Memory Of Elizabeth Reed', 'Blue Sky' and 'Ramblin' Man'.

Betts released his first solo album, *Highway* Call, in 1974 and, when the Allmans split in 1976, he resumed his solo career with *Dickey Betts And Great Southern* (1977) and *Atlanta's Burning Down* (1978). The Allman Brothers Band reformed with a revised line–up in 1978. In the mid–Nineties Betts' problems with alcohol necessitated his replacement on some dates and in 2000 he was suspended by his colleagues – a separation that became permanent. Betts re-launched his solo career, forming The Dickey Betts Band, which turned into Dickey Betts & Great Southern, playing his last ever gig in New York City on 17 December 2009, his 66th birthday. Betts originally played a 1961 Gibson SG but later replaced this with a 1957 Gibson Les Paul Goldtop, nicknamed 'Goldie'. He has also played Fender Stratocasters and PRS guitars.

### DATE OF BIRTH

12 December 1943

### PLACE OF BIRTH

West Palm Beach, USA

### GENRES

Blues Rock

# RITCHIE BLACKMORE

## RULER OF THE RIFF

Ritchie Blackmore found fame with Deep Purple, whose debut, *Shades Of Deep Purple*, was released in 1968. After a few more albums, the band released *Machine Head* (1972), one of the most influential hard-rock and heavy metal albums of all time. 'Smoke On The Water' (1973), the signature hit from the album, contains probably the most widely recognized guitar riff ever written. So powerful were Blackmore's inverted power chords that he revisited them on the later Deep Purple hits 'Woman From Tokyo' (1973) and 'Knockin' At Your Back Door' (1984).

Unhappy with the direction of the band's emerging sound, Blackmore hooked up with Ronnie James Dio and formed Rainbow in 1975. *Ritchie Blackmore's Rainbow* (1975) produced the iconic rock hit 'Man On The Silver Mountain'. In later years, Blackmore shifted Rainbow's focus to a more commercial tack, producing hits such as 'Since You've Been Gone', 'Stone Cold' and 'Street of Dreams'. In 1984 he rejoined Deep Purple and released *Perfect Strangers*, whose title track and the anthemic 'Knockin' At Your Back Door' proved that the guitarist had not lost his touch. In 1997 Blackmore formed Blackmore's Night, a primarily acoustic stew of Renaissance, folk, world and new-age music. The band of minstrels has released five studio albums and several live recordings, including the 2007 CD/DVD *Paris Moon*.

**DATE OF BIRTH**

14 April 1945

**PLACE OF BIRTH**

Weston-Super-Mare, England

**GENRES**

Rock, Heavy Metal, Renaissance, New Age, Folk

# MIKE BLOOMFIELD

## BLENDING IN WITH THE BLUES

Mike Bloomfield was an early devotee of his native Chicago's indigenous blues scene, and his empathy for blues performers saw him accepted in the South Side's largely black clubs. There he encountered CBS producer John Hammond, who signed him to the label. An equally important meeting was with harmonica player and singer Paul Butterfield, whose Paul Butterfield Blues Band Bloomfield joined in 1964. *East-West* (1966) was a groundbreaking work that saw Bloomfield hailed for his fluid lead guitar – using both a Fender Telecaster and a Gibson Les Paul – particularly on the epic, improvisational title track's blend of blues, psychedelia and Indian raga. His session work for CBS was equally groundbreaking as he accompanied Bob Dylan's first, famously controversial steps into electric rock on *Highway 61 Revisited* (1965).

Weary of touring, Bloomfield left Butterfield in 1967 to form the short–lived Electric Flag, which disbanded after one album. He teamed up with Al Kooper and made *Super Session* (1968) with Stephen Stills and *The Live Adventures Of Mike Bloomfield And Al Kooper* (1968). Bloomfield's career in the Seventies was a lower–profile affair due to his descent into drug addiction and arthritis in his hands. He died of a heroin overdose in 1981.

**DATE OF BIRTH/DEATH**

28 July 1943/15 February 1981

**PLACE OF BIRTH**

Chicago, USA

**GENRES**

Blues, Blues Rock

A-Z OF
GUITAR GODS

# BO DIDDLEY

## INFLUENTIAL RHYTHM MASTER

A pivotal figure in the transition from blues to rock'n'roll, Ellas Otha Bates secured a regular gig at the 708 Club in Chicago's South Side in 1951. Here he adopted the stage name Bo Diddley, the title of the first single he recorded in 1955. The song featured the distinctive jerky rhythm based on the 'patted juba', an African tribal beat adopted by street performers in Chicago, but known subsequently as the 'Bo Diddley beat'.

Diddley was also synonymous with his rectangular–bodied Gretsch, which he adapted himself. Nicknamed 'The Twang Machine', the guitar remained at Diddley's side throughout his career. Diddley's hard–driving rhythmic style was a major influence on the development of rock'n'roll. Songs such as 'Who Do You Love?' and 'Hey Bo Diddley' were based on one chord, de–emphasizing harmony in favour of rhythm. He made 11 albums between 1958 and 1963, while touring relentlessly. In the late Sixties he began incorporating funk into his repertoire. In 1972, he played with The Grateful Dead, and he opened for The Clash on their 1979 American tour. He remained an incalculable influence on later generations of musicians, and continued performing until his death in 2008.

### DATE OF BIRTH/DEATH

30 December 1928/2 June 2008

### PLACE OF BIRTH

McComb, USA

### GENRES

Rock'n'Roll, Blues, Funk

# PETER BUCK

## AVOIDING ROCK CLICHÉS

Alternative-rock guitarist Peter Buck met singer Michael Stipe while working in a record shop. The pair discovered that they had similar tastes in music and they joined forces with Mike Mills (bass) and Bill Berry (drums) to form R.E.M. Their debut album *Murmur* (1983) established the group's alternative credentials.

Ensuing albums – *Fables Of The Reconstruction* (1985), *Life's Rich Pageant* (1986) and *Document* (1987) – saw a move towards more traditional rock, and their major-label debut, *Green* (1988), confirmed their status as one of the first American alternative bands to cross over into the mainstream. *Out Of Time* (1991) was guitar-light but did include 'Country Feedback', an innovative combination of the guitar styles of its title. The effect was prominent again on 'Sweetness Follows' from *Automatic For The People* (1992), creating a wash of sound in place of a solo. *Monster* (1994) was a sudden leap into harder rock territory, powered by distorted, grunge-influenced guitars and glam-rock riffs. R.E.M. continued as a three-piece after the departure of Bill Berry in 1997 and four albums followed, including the guitar-driven, chart-topping *Accelerate* (2008). Buck remains most commonly associated with Rickenbacker guitars, particularly the black 'Jetglo' 360 model.

### DATE OF BIRTH

6 December 1956

### PLACE OF BIRTH

Berkeley, USA

### GENRES

Alternative Rock

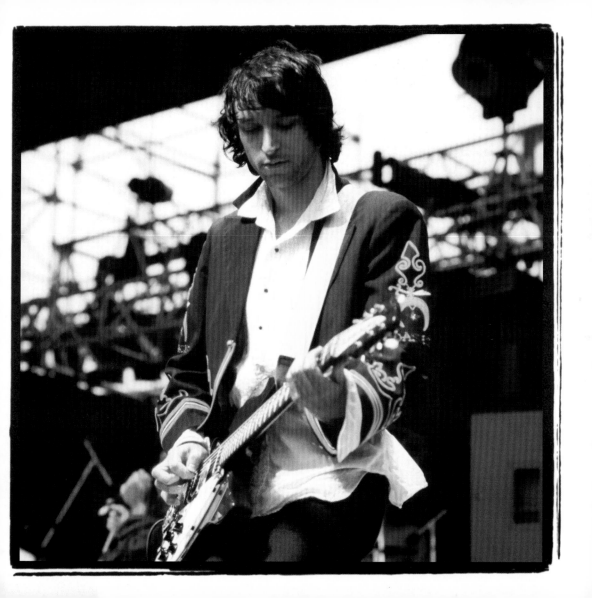

# JEFF BUCKLEY
## ECLECTIC BRILLIANCE

Son of singer–songwriter Tim, Jeff Buckley started playing acoustic guitar at the age of six and received his first electric guitar at 13. He attended the Musicians Institute in Hollywood before working in a hotel and playing in a number of bands. He moved to New York City in 1990, where he continued his musical education, taking in Qawwali (the devotional music of Pakistan), Robert Johnson and hardcore punk. His first public appearance was at a tribute concert for his father in 1991, after which he joined future collaborator Gary Lucas in Gods And Monsters before going solo. His performances at Manhattan's Sin-é club attracted intense record–company attention and he soon signed with Columbia. His eclectic guitar skills are evident on the closing tracks of debut album *Grace* (1994), where the hard–rock crunch of 'Eternal Life' is followed by the ethereal vibe of 'Dream Brother'.

Buckley was writing songs and recording demos for the follow–up when he drowned in a tragic accident in May 1997. Since then a steady reissue programme has gathered steam, including *Sketches For My Sweetheart The Drunk* (1998), which featured unfinished studio material, live compilation *Mystery White Boy* (2000) and *Songs To No One* (2002), highlighting his work with Gary Lucas. *Grace* became a posthumous bestseller as Buckley's reputation mushroomed.

**DATE OF BIRTH/DEATH**

17 November 1966/29 May 1997

**PLACE OF BIRTH**

Anaheim, USA

**GENRES**

Alternative Rock

A-Z OF GUITAR GODS

# JAMES BURTON

## CHICKEN PICKIN' MASTER

Louisiana native James Burton is one of several guitarists who parlayed his unique talent into session and tour work with rock musicians, while maintaining his ties to the country community. He first achieved local fame as a backup musician on the popular *Louisiana Hayride* radio show and got his first significant exposure with his guitar solo on Dale Hawkins' 'Suzie Q' (1957). Burton moved to California and spent six years recording and touring with teen idol Ricky Nelson, establishing him as a pop presence with distinctive guitar riffs on hits such as 'Hello Mary Lou', 'Lonesome Town' and 'Teenage Idol'.

Burton's mastery on dobro and guitar landed him studio gigs with artists as diverse as Joni Mitchell, The Monkees and Merle Haggard, often as part of the legendary LA studio band the Wrecking Crew. He worked an eight-year stint with Elvis's TCB band and then began a 16-year working relationship with John Denver, recording and touring with the singer until his death in 1997. Beginning with *King Of America* (1987), Burton recorded and toured with Elvis Costello for about a decade. He was elected to the Rock And Roll Hall Of Fame in 2001 and the Musicians Hall Of Fame in November 2007 as a member of the Wrecking Crew.

**DATE OF BIRTH**

21 August 1939

**PLACE OF BIRTH**

Minden, USA

**GENRES**

Country, Rock

# BERNARD BUTLER

## SUEDE'S CHAMELEON

Bernard Butler successfully auditioned for indie band Suede in 1989, after seeing an advertisement in *Melody Maker*. He formed a songwriting partnership with singer Brett Anderson, and together they spearheaded a shift from grunge towards a more British sound, which culminated in the Britpop phenomenon of the mid–Nineties. Butler's versatile approach was evident on their self–titled debut (1993), mixing glam–rock aggression ('Metal Mickey') and subtle touches worthy of George Harrison ('She's Not Dead'). While recording the second album, *Dog Man Star* (1994), tensions between Butler and the others escalated and he left before its completion.

He then formed McAlmont And Butler with soul singer David McAlmont. They split after two singles, but there was enough material in the can for an album *The Sound Of McAlmont And Butler* (1996). Two solo albums followed, *People Move On* (1998) and *Friends And Lovers* (1999), after which Butler renewed his partnership with Anderson. Working as the Tears, they made *Here Come The Tears* (2005), which was inevitably reminiscent of Suede. The Tears have since announced a 'temporary' hiatus, while Suede reunited for a gig in aid of Teenage Cancer Trust at London's Royal Albert Hall on 24 March 2010. Since the early days of Suede, Butler has been associated primarily with his cherry–red 1960 Gibson ES355 and also uses a black Gibson 330.

**DATE OF BIRTH**

1 May 1970

**PLACE OF BIRTH**

London, England

**GENRES**

Indie, Pop

# MAYBELLE CARTER

## THE CARTER SCRATCH

As a member of the first family of country music, Maybelle Carter (pictured left) distinguished herself far beyond her role as accompanist to her brother-in-law A.P. Carter and his wife Sara (Maybelle's cousin) in the Carter Family, the first recording stars of country music. Maybelle was the guitarist and doubled on autoharp and banjo. Her unique style involved using her thumb (with thumb-pick) to play bass and melody while her index finger filled out the rhythm on the higher strings.

In 1927, A.P. convinced Sara and Maybelle to travel to Tennessee to audition for Ralph Peer, a record producer who was looking for new talent. Later that year, a record of the group performing 'Wandering Boy' and 'Poor Orphan Child' was released. But it was 1928's release of 'The Storms Are On The Ocean' and 'Single Girl, Married Girl' that boosted the family's popularity. The Carter Family performed together until the break-up of A.P. and Sara's marriage in 1942. Maybelle continued to perform with her daughters Anita, June and Helen as Mother Maybelle & The Carter Sisters. Daughter June married country legend Johnny Cash, and Mother Maybelle & The Carter Sisters were regulars on Cash's Seventies television show. Mother Maybelle died in Nashville in 1978.

### DATE OF BIRTH/DEATH

10 May 1909/23 October 1978

### PLACE OF BIRTH

Nickelsville, USA

### GENRES

Country

A-Z OF
GUITAR GODS

# CHARLIE CHRISTIAN
## THE FiRST GREAT SOLOiST

Charlie Christian began playing around Oklahoma City in 1931. His natural talent soon attracted the attention of producer John Hammond, who drafted him into the embryonic Benny Goodman Sextet. Some reorganization followed, but Christian was retained and the group was filled out with Count Basie, trumpeter Cootie Williams and tenor-saxophonist Georgie Auld. Together they dominated the jazz polls in 1941.

More influenced by horn players such as Lester Young and Herschel Evans than by early acoustic guitarists like Eddie Lang and jazz-bluesman Lonnie Johnson, Christian admitted he wanted his guitar to sound like a tenor saxophone. By 1939 several players had adopted electric guitar, but Christian was the first great soloist. His frequent participation in after-hours jam sessions spurred the developing form of bebop, while he performed more accessible swing during his 'day job' with Goodman. Informal recordings of his late-night jamming sessions and the partial Goodman Sextet made in 1941, which included 'Blues in B' and 'Waiting for Benny', foreshadow the bop-jam sessions of the late Forties and contrast with the more formal swing music recorded after Goodman had arrived at the studio. Christian was a habitual drinker and marijuana user, and his hectic lifestyle led to his tragically early death at the age of 25.

### DATE OF BiRTH/DEATH
29 July 1916/2 March 1942
### PLACE OF BiRTH
Bonham, USA
### GENRES
Swing, Bebop, Jazz

# ERIC CLAPTON

## YARDBIRDS TO LEGEND

The most famous living guitarist in the world, Eric Clapton cut his teeth with The Yardbirds, but he moved rapidly through several bands in the Sixties. With John Mayall's Bluesbreakers he recorded the seminal blues guitar album *Bluesbreakers With Eric Clapton* (1966). Hits with supergroup Cream included *Disraeli Gears* (1967), and *Wheels Of Fire* (1968). He then formed Blind Faith with Steve Winwood, but they split after one tour.

A self-titled solo album followed, after which he formed Derek & The Dominos and released *Layla And Other Assorted Love Songs* (1970) before the band imploded in a maelstrom of drug use. Clapton was left with a heroin dependency, but he returned with the hit *461 Ocean Boulevard* (1974). Beating an alcohol dependency, Clapton confirmed his return to form with *Money And Cigarettes* (1983) and *Behind The Sun* (1985), but it was the blues that set the seal on his career. In 1992 he played the first *Unplugged* show for MTV, performing a selection of blues songs. *From The Cradle* (1994), an electric blues album, sold 10 million copies – an unprecedented feat within the genre. Since then Clapton has balanced contemporary albums (*Reptile*, 2001), with the blues (*Me And Mr Johnson*, 2004). He also revisited his past, joining John Mayall for his seventieth birthday concert in 2003, reuniting with Cream in 2005, teaming up with Winwood in 2008 and headlining London's O$_2$ Arena with former Yardbird Jeff Beck in February 2010.

### DATE OF BIRTH

30 March 1945

### PLACE OF BIRTH

Ripley, England

### GENRES

Hard Rock, Blues, Blues Rock

A-Z OF
GUITAR GODS

# KURT COBAIN

## LEADING A GENERATION

Arguably the most important alternative guitarist of the Nineties, Kurt Cobain showed a keen interest in music from an early age, singing along to Beatles' songs on the radio. Given a guitar for his fourteenth birthday, he taught himself to play along to AC/DC and The Cars. He formed Nirvana with bassist and fellow punk-rock fan Krist Novoselic, and with drummer Chad Channing the band recorded an album, *Bleach* (1989), for the local Sup Pop label. Soon afterwards Channing was replaced by Dave Grohl and in 1990 Nirvana signed to DGC Records. They recorded the crossover smash *Nevermind* (1991), which mixed abrasive guitar with pop melodies and included the genre-defining 'Smells Like Teen Spirit'. The follow-up – the booming, rumbling *In Utero* (1993) – captured the real Nirvana. Best known for his raw, angry style, Cobain was adept at acoustic work, as *Unplugged In New York* (1994) demonstrates.

The defiantly anti-establishment Cobain did not cope well with his newfound celebrity, and his life degenerated into a tabloid soap opera after his marriage to fellow rocker Courtney Love. Struggling with heroin addiction, he shot and killed himself at his home in Seattle in 1994.

**DATE OF BIRTH/DEATH**

20 February 1967/5 April 1994

**PLACE OF BIRTH**

Aberdeen, USA

**GENRES**

Grunge, Pop

# EDDIE COCHRAN

## INNOVATION PERSONIFIED

One of rock'n'roll's most influential guitarists, Eddie Cochran taught himself to play and formed his first group in high school. He later teamed up with Hank Cochran (no relation) and the duo played country music as the Cochran Brothers, and made some recordings. On seeing Elvis Presley in late 1955, Eddie was inspired to switch to rock'n'roll, and The Cochran Brothers split up soon afterwards. In 1956 Cochran recorded the Elvis–influenced 'Twenty Flight Rock' and performed it in the classic rock'n'roll movie *The Girl Can't Help It*. The following year, he recorded what would be the only LP issued in his lifetime, *Singin' To My Baby*. He went on to create three seminal rock'n'roll songs: 'C'mon Everybody', 'Somethin' Else' and 'Summertime Blues'. He was hugely popular in Britain and it was there, while on tour with Gene Vincent, that he was killed in a car crash. 'Three Steps to Heaven' became a posthumous No. 1 in Britain.

Cochran's distinctive rhythmic approach both puzzled and fascinated listeners. One of his innovations was aligning the bass and guitar to equivalent harmonic frequencies. Cochran began by using a Gibson guitar but is most closely associated with a modified 1956 Gretsch 6120 Chet Atkins Western model.

**DATE OF BIRTH/DEATH**

3 October 1938/17 April 1960

**PLACE OF BIRTH**

Albert Lea, USA

**GENRES**

Rock'n'Roll

# RY COODER

## SESSION AND SOLO SUPREMO

Versatile guitarist Ry Cooder (pictured right, beside John Lee Hooker) mastered the fundamentals of guitar as a child and, at the age of 17, played in a blues outfit with singer/songwriter Jackie DeShannon. In 1965, Cooder teamed up with Taj Mahal and Ed Cassidy in The Rising Sons, but the project fell apart when the release of their album was vetoed by CBS. Cooder then worked as a session player on many records, including Captain Beefheart & The Magic Band's first album *Safe As Milk* (1967). Cooder turned down the Captain's offer to join the band permanently and continued his session career, working with Randy Newman, Van Dyke Parks and Little Feat.

His solo debut *Ry Cooder* (1971) featured covers of blues songs, but subsequent albums explored diverse areas of American roots music. *Into The Purple Valley* (1971) embraced folk, *Chicken Skin Music* (1976) and *Showtime* (1976) blended Tex–Mex and Hawaiian, and Cooder turned his hand to Dixieland on *Jazz* (1978). *Bop Till You Drop* (1979) was more mainstream and yielded his biggest American hit, 'Little Sister'. Cooder has composed numerous soundtracks, notably the 1984 movie *Paris, Texas*, and continues to tour, playing Australia, New Zealand and Japan with Nick Lowe. Cooder's main acoustic is a Thirties Gibson Roy Smeck model. His other guitars include a Fender Stratocaster and a Gibson ES-P.

**DATE OF BIRTH**

15 March 1947

**PLACE OF BIRTH**

Los Angeles, USA

**GENRES**

American Roots, Blues, Rock

A-Z OF
GUITAR GODS

# BILLY CORGAN

## PUMPKINS' PERFECTIONIST

Self-taught alternative-rock guitarist Billy Corgan formed Smashing Pumpkins in Chicago in 1988 with James Iha (guitar) and D'Arcy Wretsky (bass). The addition of drummer Jimmy Chamberlain pumped up the band's intensity. The Pumpkins' debut album *Gish* (1991) combined hard rock and psychedelia and was recorded under difficult circumstances resulting from tensions within the band. *Siamese Dream* (1993) was similarly fraught, but it provided a breakthrough success for the Pumpkins. 'Soma' incorporated Corgan's quieter side before shifting dynamically into a wall of 40 overdubs. Other songs were reputed to contain up to 100 guitar tracks, while Corgan's squalling solos were prominent on 'Cherub Rock' and 'Quiet'. *Mellon Collie And The Infinite Sadness* (1995) was an ambitious double album. The guitars were often tuned down a half-tone as Corgan tried for a greater variety of overdubs. Its success (nine million sold) proved hard to follow and, after two more albums, Smashing Pumpkins disbanded in 2000.

Corgan formed the short-lived Zwan, whose album *Mary Star Of The Sea* (2003) was uncharacteristically upbeat and poppy. His solo album *TheFutureEmbrace* (2005) returned to alternative rock. In 2006, the Pumpkins reformed with Corgan and Chamberlain as the only original members, though the latter ended up leaving in 2009. Corgan's favourite guitar is a 1957 Fender Stratocaster.

### DATE OF BIRTH

17 March 1967

### PLACE OF BIRTH

Elk Grove Village, USA

### GENRES

Alternative Rock, Hard Rock, Psychedelia

A-Z OF
GUITAR GODS

# GRAHAM COXON

## BRINGING GUITAR INTO FOCUS

Graham Coxon was born in Germany but grew up in England. He made the acquaintance of Damon Albarn at school, and they formed Seymour (renamed Blur in 1990, on signing to indie label Food) with bassist Alex James and drummer Dave Rowntree. Their first album *Leisure* (1990) was derivative of both the 'Madchester' and 'shoe-gazing' scenes. *Modern Life Is Rubbish* (1993) reacted against grunge and American culture by celebrating Englishness. The two-million-selling *Parklife* (1994) helped to popularize what was soon dubbed 'Britpop'. The theme continued on the oddly lacklustre *The Great Escape* (1995). Their fifth album, *Blur* (1997), represented a radical change in direction, influenced by American indie-guitar bands, particularly Pavement. In this environment, Coxon's angular guitar work thrived. On *13* (1999) gospel and electronica were added to the blend.

Early in the sessions for Blur's seventh album, *Think Tank* (2003), Coxon left the band. Having already released four solo albums, his first post-Blur work and most successful solo venture was *Happiness In Magazines* (2004). Coxon plays most of the instruments on his albums and supplies the artwork for the covers. His differences with Blur have been resolved, and they performed a triumphant reunion tour in the summer of 2009, though it remains unlikely that they will work together again.

**DATE OF BIRTH**

12 March 1969

**PLACE OF BIRTH**

Rinteln, Germany

**GENRES**

Indie

# STEVE CROPPER

## THE COLONEL

Steve 'The Colonel' Cropper is an American guitarist, songwriter, producer and soul musician best known for his work creating the trailblazing soul records produced by Memphis's Stax label as a member of its studio band, which became Booker T & The MGs. Cropper started off in The Mar-Keys and had a hit single with 'Last Night' in 1961. Along with Booker T. Jones on organ and piano, bassist Donald 'Duck' Dunn and drummer Al Jackson, Jr., Cropper went on to record several hits. As a house guitarist for Stax, he played on hundreds of records, from '(Sittin' On) The Dock Of The Bay' to Sam and Dave's 'Soul Man'. Cropper also co-wrote 'Knock On Wood' with Eddie Floyd and 'In The Midnight Hour' with Wilson Pickett.

Cropper left Stax in 1970 and played on or produced records by Jeff Beck, Tower Of Power, John Prine and Jose Feliciano. He played on Ringo Starr's 1973 album *Ringo* and John Lennon's *Rock'n'Roll* (1974). In February 1998, he released *Play It, Steve!*, on which he described the inspirations behind his creation of some of soul music's most enduring songs, later releasing *Nudge It Up A Notch* (2009) with Felix Cavaliere. Cropper continues to tour and produce, recently with Australian soul singer Guy Sebastian.

**DATE OF BIRTH**

21 October 1941

**PLACE OF BIRTH**

Dora, USA

**GENRES**

Soul

# DAVE DAVIES

## THE KINKS' RIFFING LEGEND

The Davies were a musical family and Dave (pictured left) acquired his first guitar, a Harmony Meteor, at the age of 11. The Kinks came together at his secondary school, with elder brother Ray on rhythm guitar and vocals, and Pete Quaife on bass. The Kinks' third single, 'You Really Got Me', proved their breakthrough. Davies played its famous two–chord riff on his Harmony Meteor, creating the distortion effect by slashing his speaker with a razorblade.

Davies's occasional solo career got underway with the single 'Death of a Clown', which subsequently appeared on *Something Else By The Kinks* (1967). Three other singles followed, but it was not until 1980 that he issued his first solo album, *Dave Davies* (also known by its catalogue number *AF1-3603*). In the Seventies and Eighties, The Kinks became a major live attraction in America and, with Ray playing less onstage, Dave adopted a dual purpose rhythm–lead style, primarily on a Gibson L5–S. The Kinks last performed together in 1996, after which both brothers began work on solo projects. In 2004, Davies suffered a stroke, which has affected his ability to sing and play, although he has since recorded a solo album, *Fractured Mindz* (2007).

### DATE OF BIRTH

3 February 1947

### PLACE OF BIRTH

London, England

### GENRES

Rock, Pop

# DICK DALE

## SURF'S SUPERSTAR

'King of the Surf Guitar' Dick Dale learned to play drums, ukulele and trumpet before taking up the guitar. He began playing in clubs, solo at first but later backed by The Del-Tones. His recording career began in 1961 with the single 'Let's Go Trippin'', regarded as the first surf-rock song, and he achieved national popularity in the States with *Surfer's Choice* (1962). After almost losing a leg to a surfing injury sustained in polluted water, he became an environmental activist. He is best known for 'Misirlou' (1962), which brought him to a new audience in the Nineties when used in the movie *Pulp Fiction* and which led to his comeback as a recording artist.

Dale is left-handed but learned to play on a right-handed guitar without restringing it, effectively playing the instrument upside down. He was notorious for using strings of the heaviest gauge possible but still regularly breaking them and wearing out plectrums because of his forceful playing. He aimed to recreate the experiences of surfing in his guitar playing; his trademark twang was intended to simulate the sound of the waves breaking. He uses a signature-model Stratocaster, given to him by Fender.

**DATE OF BIRTH**

4 May 1937

**PLACE OF BIRTH**

Boston, USA

**GENRES**

Surf Rock

# PACO DE LUCÍA

## FLAMENCO FLAIR

In 1958, at the age of 11, Paco de Lucía made his first public appearance on Radio Algeciras, and a year later he was awarded a special prize in the Jerez flamenco competition. In 1961, he toured with the flamenco troupe of dancer José Greco. In 1964 de Lucía met Madrilenian guitarist Ricardo Modrego, with whom he recorded *Dos Guitarras Flamencas* (1965) and *Doce Canciones De Federico García Lorca Para Guitarra* (1965). Between 1968 and 1977, he enjoyed a fruitful collaboration with fellow new–flamenco innovator Camarón de la Isla, with whom he recorded 10 albums.

In 1979, de Lucía, John McLaughlin and Larry Coryell formed The Guitar Trio. Coryell was later replaced by Al Di Meola, and the group recorded *Friday Night In San Francisco* (1980) and *The Guitar Trio* (1996), with that line–up. His own band, The Paco De Lucía Sextet (which includes his brothers Ramón and Pepe) released the first of their three albums that same year. De Lucía has released several albums encompassing both traditional and modern flamenco styles. He introduced instruments, techniques and variations that shocked flamenco purists yet became accepted elements of the modern musical form. Other important works include *Siroco* (1988), *Luzia* (1998) and *Cositas Buena*s (2004).

**DATE OF BIRTH**

21 December 1947

**PLACE OF BIRTH**

Algeciras, Spain

**GENRES**

Flamenco, Classical, Jazz, Funk, World

A–Z OF
GUITAR GODS

# AL DI MEOLA
## A TECHNICAL MAESTRO

Contemporary jazz guitarist Al Di Meola joined Chick Corea's band, Return To Forever, in 1974. It was here that he was first noted for his technical mastery and fast, complex guitar solos and compositions. Di Meola built on his reputation with his first solo album, *Land Of The Midnight Sun* (1976). He branched out to explore Mediterranean cultures and acoustic genres on cuts such as 'Mediterranean Sundance' and 'Lady Of Rome'. He showed his range on acoustic numbers – 'Fantasia Suite For Two Guitars' from the *Casino* (1978) album, for instance, and on the bestselling live album *Friday Night In San Francisco* (1980). With *Scenario* (1983), he explored the electronic side of jazz in a collaboration with Jan Hammer. He broadened his acoustic sensibilities on *Cielo E Terra* (1985) and incorporated guitar/synthesizers on albums such as *Soaring Through A Dream* (1985).

In the Nineties, Di Meola moved into ethnic and world music and explored modern Latin styles. He mixed acoustic and guitar–synthesizer pieces with a selection of electric guitar numbers. Di Meola has been more active on acoustic guitar in recent years. He played a series of dates with Return To Forever's mid–Seventies line–up of Chick Corea, Stanley Clarke and Lenny White in 2008.

### DATE OF BIRTH

22 July 1954

### PLACE OF BIRTH

Jersey City, USA

### GENRES

Jazz, Jazz Fusion, Latin Jazz

# NICK DRAKE

## TALENT AND TRAGEDY

The acoustic guitarist and singer–songwriter Nick Drake was a tragic figure in the English folk–rock community. His beautiful if bleak songs only became fully appreciated decades after his death from an overdose of anti–depressant medication. He was discovered by Fairport Convention bassist Ashley Hutchings, and signed to Island Records when he was 20 years old. He released *Five Leaves Left* (1969), *Bryter Layter* (1970) and *Pink Moon* (1972), but none of the albums sold well, and Drake's increasing reluctance to perform live or help promote the albums crippled their chances. After *Pink Moon* he sank into depression, retreating to his parents' home, where he died in 1974.

Interest in Drake's music grew through the mid–Seventies, but it was not until Island's release of the retrospective album *Fruit Tree* (1979) that his back catalogue came to be reassessed. In 1985 The Dream Academy reached the UK and US charts with its Drake tribute 'Life In A Northern Town'. In 1998 the documentary film *A Stranger Amongst Us* brought Drake more fans, and in 2000 Volkswagen featured the title track from *Pink Moon* in a television advertisement. Within a month Drake had sold more records than he had in the previous 30 years.

### DATE OF BIRTH/DEATH

19 June 1948/25 November 1974

### PLACE OF BIRTH

Rangoon, Burma (Myanmar)

### GENRES

Folk Rock

# DUANE EDDY

## THE REBEL ROUSER

While playing guitar in a country duo, Duane Eddy met songwriter, producer and disc jockey Lee Hazelwood. The pair embarked on a writing and production partnership, pioneering the rock'n'roll instrumental. 'Movin'' 'n' Groovin'' was a minor hit for Eddy in 1958, followed by the Top 10 success of 'Rebel Rouser'. Eddy's chart success started to dry up in 1962, but he remained an active and innovative performer, recording many albums and branching out into producing and acting. He returned to the British charts in 1975 with 'Play Me Like You Play Your Guitar'. In 1986 he recorded a new version of 'Peter Gunn' with avant-garde outfit Art of Noise. The album *Duane Eddy* (1987) followed. It featured guest appearances by many of the musicians he had influenced, including Paul McCartney, George Harrison, Jeff Lynne, Ry Cooder and John Fogerty.

Eddy was the first rock'n'roll guitarist with a signature model, the Guild DE-400 and deluxe DE-500. For a long time, he was associated with the Gretsch Chet Atkins 6120. He achieved his unique twangy guitar sound by bending the bass strings and using a combination of echo chamber and tremolo arm.

**DATE OF BIRTH**

26 April 1938

**PLACE OF BIRTH**

Corning, USA

**GENRES**

Rock'n'Roll, Country

# THE EDGE

## SEARCHING FOR SONIC MEANING

David Evans met the others members of the band that became U2 – Larry Mullen, Jr., Paul Hewson (Bono) and Adam Clayton – at school in Dublin, and he soon adopted the moniker by which he is now known. The band's initial release, *Boy* (1980), won positive reviews and by *War* (1984) U2 were gaining international attention. In search of a new sound, they enlisted the unconventional talents of Brian Eno and Daniel Lanois for *The Unforgettable Fire* (1984), which spawned the hit 'Pride (In the Name of Love)' and solidified U2's following in the US. *The Joshua Tree* (1987) became the fastest–selling album in British chart history.

The band have continued a phenomenal pattern of releasing albums – *Achtung Baby* (1991), *All That You Can't Leave Behind* (2000), *How To Dismantle An Atomic Bomb* (2004) – followed by increasingly elaborate tours, the latest of which was the U2 360° tour, launched in 2009 to support that year's *No Line On The Horizon*. It is in part the band's obsession with freshness that has established U2 as one of the greatest bands in rock history. Crucial to this achievement has been The Edge's search for sonic meaning as he crafted a guitar sound with delays, reverbs and a minimalist approach to playing that complemented the passion, pain and joy embedded in U2's music.

**DATE OF BIRTH**

8 August 1961

**PLACE OF BIRTH**

London, England

**GENRES**

Rock, Pop

A–Z OF
GUITAR GODS

# TIM FARRISS

## MASTER OF THE UNDERSTATED

Tim Farriss found fame with his brothers Andrew and Jon as a member of INXS, originally known as The Farriss Brothers Band. Adding guitarist and saxophonist Kirk Pengilly and lead singer Michael Hutchence, the band released its debut album, *INXS*, in 1980, followed by *Underneath The Colours* in 1981, both of which found success in their native Australia. *The Swing* (1984) brought the band its international reputation, and 'Original Sin' became their first No. 1. 'Original Sin' didn't fare as well in the UK, though, and INXS had only marginal success on the charts until 1987 with the release of *Kick* (reaching 3 in the US charts, and 9 in the UK), having perfected their Rolling Stones- and Chic-influenced style on 1985's *Listen Like Thieves*.

Farriss became known as a versatile guitarist who could move smoothly from the funk-influenced style of INXS's early works to the crunchy grooves of their hard-rock material; a master of the understated, tasty riff more than the flamboyant solo. Farriss suffered from bone disease and injuries throughout his life, but always recovered to lend his defining guitar work to the band throughout their 25-year history. INXS gained new attention in 2005 with a reality-based TV show 'Rock Star: INXS', in which they chose a new lead singer for their first new album in eight years, *Switch*; and in 2010 they performed at the Vancouver Winter Olympics.

**DATE OF BIRTH**

16 August 1957

**PLACE OF BIRTH**

Perth, Australia

**GENRES**

Rock, Pop

# PETER FRAMPTON

## LEGEND COMES ALIVE

Peter Frampton took classical guitar lessons as a child, but by the age of 10 he was playing rock'n'roll and by his mid-teens was in The Preachers, who were produced and managed by Bill Wyman. By 1966 he was lead singer and guitarist in The Herd, with whom he scored a handful of British hits. In 1969 he co-founded Humble Pie and went on to record five albums before leaving to concentrate on a solo career. He released four solo albums between 1972 and 1975, and his buzz began to build through non-stop touring. His show was released in February 1976 as *Frampton Comes Alive!*. Within months, Frampton was the biggest pop-rock star in the world.

Frampton was pressured to quickly record a follow-up, and *I'm In You* (1977) was deemed a disappointment. Then the film *Sergeant Pepper's Lonely Hearts Club Band* (1978), in which Frampton starred, flopped. He suffered a near-fatal car accident in the Bahamas and descended into drug dependency. He never regained his previous popularity, but continued to record and tour. Frampton never lost his dedication to guitar. In 2006 he released an all-instrumental work, *Fingerprints*, which won the Grammy for Best Pop Instrumental Album in 2007. *Thank You Mr Churchill* was released in April 2010.

**DATE OF BIRTH**

22 April 1950

**PLACE OF BIRTH**

Beckenham, England

**GENRES**

Rock, Pop Rock, Hard Rock, Blues

# MARTY FRIEDMAN

## SHREDDING SUPERSTAR

Best-known as the shred guitarist for metal giants Megadeath, Martin 'Marty' Friedman signed with Shrapnel Records in 1982. Five years later he recorded *Speed Metal Symphony* under the moniker Cacophony with Jason Becker. It was a hit in the shred community, and Friedman's solo debut, *Dragon's Kiss*, followed a year later, in 1988. The exposure, combined with Friedman's virtuosity, led to his joining thrash giants Megadeth in 1990. Their first album together, *Rust In Peace* (1990), is generally recognized as one of the most technically accomplished thrash albums in history. His second album with Megadeth, *Countdown To Extinction* (1992), further demonstrated the unique chemistry that had seemingly eluded singer/leader Dave Mustaine for most of his career, thanks in large part again to Friedman's fretwork.

Around this time, Friedman began to seek out additional outlets for his non-metal, exotic compositions. He formed a partnership with new-age musician Kitaro and released the Asian-themed instrumental record *Scenes* (1992). In the coming years, he released two other solo-guitar albums in the same vein, before recording his final album with Megadeth, *Risk*, in 1999. Since then he has moved to Japan, where he continues to record exotic rock instrumental guitar albums, the most recent being *Loudspeaker* (2006), alongside Japanese covers albums such as 2009's *Tokyo Jukebox*.

**DATE OF BIRTH**

8 December 1962

**PLACE OF BIRTH**

Washington, DC, USA

**GENRES**

Rock, Heavy Metal, Shred

# ROBERT FRIPP

## CRIMSON'S KING

Despite being tone-deaf, left-handed and possessing a poor sense of rhythm, Robert Fripp picked up the guitar at age 11 and never looked back. In 1967 he teamed up with brothers Peter (bass) and Michael Giles (drums) to form Giles, Giles & Fripp. A year later, Fripp and Michael Giles formed the first version of King Crimson. Their debut album, *In The Court Of The Crimson King* (1969), proved enormously influential. Indeed, throughout the band's on-and-off existence, albums such as *Red* (1974), *Discipline* (1981) and *The Power To Believe* (2003) have continued to demonstrate Fripp's ability to create ambitious and innovative music.

Fripp has worked with many artists as sideman and collaborator through the years, including Brian Eno, David Bowie, Talking Heads, Andy Summers and Peter Gabriel. With Eno, Fripp developed his famous 'Frippertronics' – a sound-on-sound live tape-looping process that enables him to become his own backing track. He recently introduced his 'soundscapes' approach to legions of new fans on the 2004 G3 tour. Fripp also launched Guitar Craft in 1985, a guitar seminar programme that holds ongoing instructional courses all over the world, teaching hundreds of guitarists the eccentric, trippy, inventive and dissonant, yet somehow melodic, craft of the renowned master.

**DATE OF BIRTH**

16 May 1946

**PLACE OF BIRTH**

Wimbourne Minster, England

**GENRES**

Progressive Rock

A-Z OF
GUITAR GODS

# BILL FRISELL

## SENSATIONAL SESSION STAR

Bill Frisell built an eclectic career creating guitar music in several disciplines and genres. His major break came when Pat Metheny recommended him to drummer Paul Motian for a session. Motian's label, ECM Records, made Frisell its in-house guitar player. His first solo release was *In Line* (1983), with contributions from bassist Arild Andersen, and throughout the Eighties Frisell worked with many others in New York. In the early Nineties Frisell made two of his best-known albums: *Have A Little Faith* (1992), an ambitious album tackling Charles Ives and Aaron Copland ('Billy The Kid'), John Hiatt (the title song), Bob Dylan ('Just Like A Woman') and Madonna ('Live To Tell'); and *This Land* (1992), a complementary set of originals.

In the mid-Nineties, Frisell provided music for the TV version of 'The Far Side'. It was released on the album *Quartet* (1996) along with music written for Keaton's 'Convict'. Some of Frisell's songs, including 'Over The Rainbow' and 'Coffaro's Theme', were featured in the movie *Finding Forrester* (2000). He won the 2005 Grammy Award for Best Contemporary Jazz Album for his album *Unspeakable*. Frisell uses an array of effects, including delay, distortion, reverb, octave shifters and volume pedals to create unique textures.

### DATE OF BIRTH

18 March 1951

### PLACE OF BIRTH

Baltimore, USA

### GENRES

Jazz, Progressive Folk, Classical, Country, Noise

A-Z OF GUITAR GODS

# JOHN FRUSCIANTE
## MELODIC MAESTRO

Alt–rock guitarist John Frusciante became involved with New York's punk–rock scene as a young teenager and was particularly inspired by The Germs, teaching himself to play the songs on their first album before taking guitar lessons. He became a devotee of Red Hot Chili Peppers, learning the guitar parts from their first three albums, as performed by the band's lead guitarist Hillel Slovak. When Slovak died from a heroin overdose in 1988, Frusciante successfully auditioned to replace his role model. His second album with the Chili Peppers, *Blood Sugar Sex Magik* (1991), was a big seller, finally turning the band into stars, but Frusciante was unable to handle the newfound success and quit in May 1992. Struggling with depression, he turned to drugs and alcohol but, by 1998, he had cleaned up. In this year he rejoined the Chili Peppers when his replacement Dave Navarro was fired, leaving again in 2009, the same year that he released his tenth solo album, *The Empyrean*.

Frusciante is an emotional and melodic guitarist, and emphasizes these qualities over virtuosity. Nevertheless, he possesses great technical ability, and many of his live solos are improvised. He prefers pre–1970 guitars for their sonic qualities and selects the most appropriate instrument for the song; but his most frequently played guitar is a 1962 Sunburst Fender Stratocaster.

### DATE OF BIRTH

5 March 1970

### PLACE OF BIRTH

New York, USA

### GENRES

Alternative Rock, Indie, Electronica

# NOEL GALLAGHER

## BRITPOP'S TRAILBLAZER

Britpop guitarist Noel Gallagher began teaching himself guitar at the age of 13 and later became a roadie for Manchester indie band Inspiral Carpets. Returning in 1992 from an American tour, he discovered younger brother Liam singing in a band, Rain, with Paul 'Bonehead' Arthurs (guitar), Paul McGuigan (bass) and Tony McCarroll (drums). Noel agreed to join as long as he could take creative control. Renamed Oasis, the band's rise was swift, graduating to stadium gigs within two years of the release of their debut single 'Supersonic' in 1994.

Oasis's first album, *Definitely Maybe* (1994), was steeped in rock classicism with echoes of the Sex Pistols. New drummer Alan White joined for *(What's The Story) Morning Glory?* (1995), and his skills enabled Oasis to craft a more varied, Beatles-influenced collection, with Noel's strident lead on the title track and adroit acoustic work on 'Wonderwall' particularly notable. Gallagher favours Epiphone Sheratons and has a signature blue 'Supernova' model. Although naturally left-handed, he plays right-handed. The Gallagher brothers' pursuit of the rock'n'roll lifestyle resulted in an overproduced third album, *Be Here Now* (1997), but the group subsequently recovered some of their early form, notably with the critically acclaimed *Dig Out Your Soul* (2008). In August 2009, Noel quit the band just minutes before they were due on stage at Paris's Rock en Seine festival, following an argument with Liam. The future of the unnamed Liam-led group remains uncertain.

### DATE OF BIRTH

29 May 1967

### PLACE OF BIRTH

Manchester, England

### GENRES

Rock, Britpop

A-Z OF
GUITAR GODS

# RORY GALLAGHER

## KEEPING THE FAITH

Respected blues guitarist Rory Gallagher formed the power trio Taste in 1966, with whom he released two studio and two live albums. Shortly after their appearance at the 1970 Isle of Wight Festival, Taste split acrimoniously. Gallagher, already an established virtuoso, went solo. Throughout the Seventies he produced 10 albums: *Live In Europe* (1972) captured his high-octane live show, and a second live album, *Irish Tour* (1974), sold in excess of two million copies worldwide. His later output was more sporadic, but he remained a hugely popular live attraction and toured constantly. He died in 1995 after years of ill-health.

Gallagher was closely identified with his sunburst Fender Stratocaster, which he bought in 1961, impressed with its appearance and swayed by Buddy Holly's use of the same model. The Strat was invaluable to Gallagher for its bright tone and because he could achieve a wah-wah effect by manipulating its tone control rather than using a pedal. Soloing on the Stratocaster, Gallagher created an exquisite flurry of notes on 'Daughter of the Everglades' from *Blueprint* (1973). A Martin D-35 was his favoured acoustic. Gallagher's bottleneck technique was widely admired by his peers and was showcased on the title track of *Calling Card* (1976).

### DATE OF BIRTH/DEATH

2 March 1948/14 June 1995

### PLACE OF BIRTH

Ballyshannon, Ireland

### GENRES

Blues, Rock, Blues Rock

# JERRY GARCIA
## GRATEFUL'S GREATNESS

A leading figure on America's West-Coast music scene, Jerry Garcia was inspired to learn guitar by the music of Chuck Berry, Buddy Holly and Eddie Cochran. In the early Sixties, he met future Grateful Dead bassist Phil Lesh and lyricist Robert Hunter. He began performing in a bluegrass outfit and subsequently a jug band, which evolved into The Warlocks and ultimately The Grateful Dead. The band fused many diverse elements – psychedelia, bluegrass, folk, blues and country – all of which were evident in Garcia's extended solos. Their commercially successful albums, *Workingman's Dead* and *American Beauty* (both 1970) featured more conventional, country-flavoured musicianship. Although the Dead gigged relentlessly, Garcia found time for extra-curricular activity, notably The Jerry Garcia Band, some Grateful Dead spin-offs and sessions for other musicians such as Crosby, Stills, Nash & Young, Jefferson Airplane and New Riders of the Purple Sage. After struggling with heroin addiction for many years, Garcia died of a heart attack in 1995.

Throughout his career, Garcia used a variety of guitars, sometimes favouring the Gibson SG or Les Paul, at other times the Fender Stratocaster. In 1973, he acquired his first custom-built guitar, and later added two more, all from the guitar and bass company Alembic.

### DATE OF BIRTH/DEATH
1 August 1942/9 August 1995

### PLACE OF BIRTH
San Francisco, USA

### GENRES
Psychedlia, Rock'n'Roll, Bluegrass, Folk Rock, R&B, Country Rock

# BiLLY GiBBONS

## ZZ TOP'S TALENT

Billy F. Gibbons, also known as the Reverend Willie G, began in The Moving Sidewalks, which recorded *Flash* (1968) and opened for The Jimi Hendrix Experience during the Texas leg of Hendrix's first American tour. Gibbons formed ZZ Top in late 1969 and released *ZZ Top's First Album* in 1971. The follow–ups, *Rio Grande Mud* (1972) and *Tres Hombres* (1973), combined with extensive touring, cemented the band's reputation as a hard–rocking power trio. It was in the Eighties, however, that ZZ Top really exploded, creating their three biggest albums, *Eliminator* (1983), *Afterburner* (1985) and *Recycler* (1990). A series of videos for the hit singles 'Legs', 'Gimme All Your Lovin'', and 'Sharp Dressed Man', among others, became staples of the young music video channel MTV.

Although ZZ Top lost some of their early fans with their more radio–friendly sound and missteps such as the effects–laden remixed box set *Six Pack* (1987), the band's unique blend of boogie and funny, sometimes raunchy, lyrics, anchored by Gibbons' blues–based virtuosity, continued to draw fans. In recent years Gibbons has made appearances with other bands and acted on television shows. The *Eliminator Collector's Edition* CD/DVD celebrating the 25th anniversary of the album was released in 2008, while a new album, rumoured since 2006, is yet to be released.

### DATE OF BIRTH

16 December 1949

### PLACE OF BIRTH

Houston, USA

### GENRES

Hard Rock, Blues Rock

# PAUL GILBERT

## RACER X'S MR BIG

Irreverent shred guitarist Paul Gilbert sent a tape of his band Missing Lynx to Shrapnel Records' head Mike Varney in 1982, and Varney immediately put Gilbert into his Spotlight column in *Guitar Player* magazine. In 1984 Gilbert met the future members of Racer X at the Guitar Institute of Technology. The band recorded their debut album, *Street Lethal*, in 1985 and Gilbert was soon one of the most talked-about guitarists on the scene. By the time they released their second album, *Second Heat* (1987), they were selling out all the big clubs on the LA scene.

Whereas Racer X was essentially one giant adrenaline rush, Gilbert's next band, Mr Big, offered him the opportunity to stretch his songwriting wings, and the band's 1989 self-titled debut reached No. 46 on the *Billboard* Top 200 album chart. But it was 1991's *Lean Into It*, featuring the No. 1 acoustic ballad 'To Be With You', that brought Gilbert more widespread acclaim. In 1997, Gilbert left Mr Big to pursue a solo career. He has since released 10 studio albums, including his first-ever all-instrumental record, *Get Out Of My Yard* (2006). His signature-model Ibanez PGM guitars and his instructional videos continue to be top sellers.

**DATE OF BIRTH**

6 November 1966

**PLACE OF BIRTH**

Carbondale, USA

**GENRES**

Hard Rock, Heavy Metal, Shred

A-Z OF
GUITAR GODS

# DAVID GILMOUR

## PINK FLOYD PIONEER

In 1968, David Gilmour was asked by childhood friend Roger Waters to join Pink Floyd to cover for the increasingly erratic Syd Barrett. The band had started work on their second album, *A Saucerful Of Secrets* (1968), and Gilmour helped structure the 12–minute instrumental title track. His strong, clean tone, blended with an increasing variety of effects pedals, became features of ensuing albums, and his carefully constructed guitar parts were a distinctive element of the Pink Floyd sound defined on *The Dark Side Of The Moon* (1973). He developed his sound further on *Wish You Were Here* (1975) but by *The Wall* (1979) his scope was becoming limited by Waters' control, and he began to focus on solo work.

In 1986 Waters quit and Gilmour and the others released *A Momentary Lapse Of Reason* in 1987. They embarked on a world tour that ran for three years and yielded the live *Delicate Sound Of Thunder* (1988). *The Division Bell* (1994) found Gilmour writing most of the music, and the subsequent world tour produced another live album, *Pulse* (1995). Gilmour then resumed his solo career, playing acoustic concerts in London and Paris in 2001 and 2002. He released his third solo album, *On An Island*, in 2006, having played with a reformed Pink Floyd at 2005's Live 8.

### DATE OF BIRTH

6 March 1946

### PLACE OF BIRTH

Cambridge, England

### GENRES

Progressive Rock, Blues Rock, Hard Rock, Psychedelic Rock

# PETER GREEN

## FLEETWOOD MAC'S FOUNDER

Blues-rock guitarist Peter Green played bass in several semi-pro outfits before keyboardist Peter Bardens invited him to play lead in his band. Three months later, he joined John Mayall's Bluesbreakers, replacing Eric Clapton. Green quickly established himself, developing an economical, sweetly melancholic style on his favoured Gibson Les Paul. The Bluesbreaker album *Hard Road* (1967) contains two Green compositions, including the instrumental 'The Supernatural'. His next band utilized Bluesbreakers' rhythm section Mick Fleetwood (drums) and John McVie (bass), with Jeremy Spencer (slide guitar, vocals) and Green on lead and vocals. Debut album *Fleetwood Mac* (1968) was a mix of blues classics and original material. *Mr Wonderful* (1968) was straight-ahead blues, recorded live in the studio, and the No. 1 single that year, 'Albatross', showcased Green's stately, mournful blues playing.

Green struggled with fame, and his personality changed after a bad LSD trip. He left Fleetwood Mac in 1970, released a solo album, *The End Of The Game*, the same year, and then disappeared, taking a succession of menial jobs and spending time in mental institutions. He re-emerged as a recording artist in 1979 but relapsed in 1984. He made another comeback in the Nineties in the Peter Green Splinter Group, making nine albums up to 2003, and resumed touring again with Peter Green And Friends in 2009.

### DATE OF BIRTH

29 October 1946

### PLACE OF BIRTH

London, England

### GENRES

Rock, Blues Rock

A-Z OF
GUITAR GODS

# JONNY GREENWOOD
## RADIOHEAD TO GUITAR HERO

The lead guitarist in Radiohead, Jonny Greenwood met the other members of the band in 1986. Their first album, *Pablo Honey* (1993), blended guitar-led anthemic rock with atmospheric instrumental passages. *The Bends* (1995) was a constrastingly low-key album of melancholic grandeur full of dense guitar arrangements. *OK Computer* (1997) was a minimalist art-rock album that changed the face of Nineties music. Greenwood used a wide range of sounds and effects to enhance the songs, from smooth, sliding tones, through squeaks and wails, to complex, spacey sounds.

*Kid A* (2000) deliberately moved away from conventional melodies and guitars were less in evidence, although Greenwood's guitar was prominent on 'Optimistic' – the closest the band got to a pop song on that album. *Amnesiac* (2001) had a lighter feel, but the guitars were mostly used for ambient textures. *In Rainbows* (2007) restored the passion in the studio that Radiohead had never lost on stage, with guitars making a telling contribution to '15 Steps', 'Bodysnatchers' and 'Jigsaw Falling into Place'. Greenwood also released a solo album, *Bodysong* (2003), a documentary soundtrack that featured guitars on just two tracks, as he focused on his multi-instrument and arranging skills; and scored the soundtrack for the 2007 film *There Will Be Blood*. In 2004 he was appointed composer in residence at the BBC, while Radiohead are currently working on new material, releasing songs online.

**DATE OF BIRTH**

5 November 1971

**PLACE OF BIRTH**

Oxford, England

**GENRES**

Art Rock

A-Z OF
GUITAR GODS

# GUITAR SLIM

## HIGH-VOLTAGE HERO

In his brief career, Guitar Slim electrified the blues in more ways than one. While most bluesmen didn't alter their style as they moved from acoustic to electric guitar, Slim developed a uniquely electric style, creating a sustained whining note that was a revelation in his time. His live shows were equally high-voltage. Often dressed in a cherry-red suit, he would begin playing offstage before making his entrance on the shoulders of a burly minder.

Born Eddie Jones in Greenwood, Mississippi, Slim worked in the cotton fields before he began singing and dancing with local bands. He later moved down to New Orleans, forming a band with Huey 'Piano' Smith and working up his flamboyant stage show. He hit the jackpot in 1954 with the swampy, gospel-flavoured 'The Things I Used To Do'. It was the bestselling rhythm and blues record for 14 consecutive weeks and reached No. 23 in the pop charts. However, none of his attempts at a follow-up – including the soulful 'Sufferin' Mind', and 'Something To Remember You By', or the rocking 'Letter To My Girlfriend' and 'It Hurts To Love Someone' – managed any kind of chart success and he died in 1959, a victim of his hard-drinking lifestyle.

### DATE OF BIRTH/DEATH

10 December 1926/7 February 1959

### PLACE OF BIRTH

Greenwood, USA

### GENRES

Blues, Rock'n'Roll .

# BUDDY GUY

## LEGEND OF LIVE LICKS

George 'Buddy' Guy was born in Louisiana and started playing in and around Baton Rouge in his teens. In 1957 he moved to Chicago, where he was encouraged by his idol, Muddy Waters, and developed his own style – a mixture of the showmanship of Guitar Slim and the rapid–fire phrasing of B.B. King. He signed with Chess in 1960, and his first session produced the harrowing 'First Time I Met The Blues'. He scored a hit with 'Stone Crazy' in 1962, but most of his own recordings remained unreleased. His first British visit in 1965 with the American Folk Blues Festival launched his prestigious fan club. He also started a long–lasting and fruitful relationship with harmonica player and singer Junior Wells. The duo played together on *Hoodoo Man Blues* (1965) and *Play The Blues* (1972) among others.

The Seventies and Eighties were a lean period for Buddy Guy recordings and it wasn't until *Damn Right I've Got The Blues* (1991), followed by *Feels Like Rain* (1993) and *Slippin' In* (1995) – all Grammy winners – that he started achieving commercial success. Guy has had a long relationship with Fender, preferring to play a Stratocaster through a Fender Tweed Bassman (4 x 10).

### DATE OF BIRTH

30 July 1936

### PLACE OF BIRTH

Lettsworth, USA

### GENRES

Blues, R&B, Chicago Blues

A-Z OF
GUITAR GODS

# STEVE HACKETT

## GUITAR GENIUS AND GENESIS

Steve Hackett joined Genesis in 1970 and his introspective manner and controlled guitar effects played out well on a succession of albums, including *Nursery Cryme* (1971), *Selling England By The Pound* (1973) and *The Lamb Lies Down On Broadway* (1974). In 1975 he released the solo *Voyage Of The Acolyte*, which expanded on areas he had touched on in Genesis. The next Genesis album, *A Trick Of The Tail* (1976), marked a new beginning for the band, but Hackett grew dissatisfied with the level of his contribution and left the group in 1977.

His second solo album, *Please Don't Touch* (1978), was deliberately diverse. *Spectral Mornings* (1979) focused on Hackett's own identity, with powerful guitar playing on 'Every Day'. *Cured* (1981) and *Highly Strung* (1983) saw a move towards the pop mainstream, but Hackett still consciously varied the style of his albums. *Bay Of Kings* (1983) focused on his acoustic playing and *Till We Have Faces* (1984) was recorded in Brazil with Latin percussionists. Since the Nineties his albums have switched between acoustic and electric, and include the contemporary *Guitar Noir* (1993), the R&B–based *Blues With A Feeling* (1994) and *Sketches Of Satie* (2000), which featured arrangements for guitar and flute played by his brother John. His 2009 album, *Out The Tunnel's Mouth*, finally saw release, following legal issues leading up to its release date. Hackett's favourite guitar is a 1957 Gibson Les Paul Goldtop.

### DATE OF BIRTH

12 February 1950

### PLACE OF BIRTH

London, England

### GENRES

Progressive Rock, Hard Rock, Pop

# KIRK HAMMETT

## METALLICA'S MASTER OF GUITAR

Kirk Hammett was weaned on his older brother's extensive hard-rock record collection, which included albums by Jimi Hendrix, Led Zeppelin and UFO. Inspired, Hammett picked up a Montgomery Ward catalogue guitar, hooked up with vocalist Paul Baloff and formed Exodus. The pioneering thrash band later supported Metallica and in 1983 he was invited to join the group. It wasn't long before Hammett had made a name for himself in the guitar community via his incendiary scalar lines in solos such as 'Fade To Black' from 1984's *Ride The Lightning*. Two years later, in 1986, the band released what many believe to be their magnum opus, *Master Of Puppets*.

In 1987, Hammett began a long and fruitful association with ESP guitars. With his signature guitar in hand, Hammett laid down some of his scariest lines to date on Metallica's 1988 release, *...And Justice For All*. But it was the band's 1991 self-titled release that enshrined Metallica as the reigning kings of metal. Ironically, while the band finally achieved mass commercial success, Hammett's bluesier, wah-drenched soloing approach saw his stock among some in the guitar community drop. But his 2007 endorsement deal with Randall amplifiers and ESP's limited-run 20th anniversary Kirk Hammett model guitar proves that he maintains his relevancy, while Metallica's 2008 album, *Death Magnetic*, was largely hailed as a return to form.

**DATE OF BIRTH**

18 November 1962

**PLACE OF BIRTH**

San Francisco, USA

**GENRES**

Heavy Metal, Thrash Metal

A-Z OF GUITAR GODS

# GEORGE HARRISON

## BEATLEMANIA

Influenced by Lonnie Donegan, Carl Perkins and Chet Atkins, Harrison was already developing a unique style when he joined John Lennon's Quarrymen and became part of rock history. As a songwriter he grew slowly from the telling solitude of 'Don't Bother Me' to the universality of 'Something' and 'Here Comes The Sun'. As a guitarist he often deferred to the wishes of Paul McCartney and producer George Martin, but his carefully crafted solos and his exposure with the Beatles inspired millions to take up guitar, while making the Gretsch Country Gentleman and Rickenbacker 360 12-string two of the world's most recognized instruments.

Harrison exposed the western world to the sitar and brought exotic sounds to The Beatles' records as they shifted their focus from live performing to studio work. As a solo artist Harrison was the first ex-Beatle to score a major hit with his three-disc *All Things Must Pass*. He adopted a signature slide-guitar sound and branched out with work as a humanitarian (*The Concert For Bangladesh*), filmmaker (Handmade Films) and band mate (the Traveling Wilburys). He left a legacy of guitar music that justified his 2004 entry as a solo artist into the Rock And Roll Hall Of Fame.

### DATE OF BIRTH/DEATH

25 February 1943/29 November 2001

### PLACE OF BIRTH

Liverpool, England

### GENRES

Pop, Rock

# EDDIE HAZEL

## THE HERO OF FUNK

Eddie Hazel played guitar and sang in church as a child. At the age of 12, he met Billy 'Bass' Nelson, and the pair sang and played guitar together. In 1967 George Clinton of the doo-wop band The Parliaments recruited them for the back-up band. While on tour Hazel met and befriended Tiki Fulwood, who replaced The Parliaments' drummer. Nelson, Hazel and Fulwood became the core of Funkadelic, the new name for The Parliaments. In short order the group recorded *Funkadelic* (1970) and *Free Your Mind ... And Your Ass Will Follow* (1970). The title track of the third album, *Maggot Brain* (1971), featuring Hazel's 10-minute guitar solo, cemented his reputation.

Drug problems led Clinton to suspend Hazel's salary, and the guitarist had only a small role on *America Eats Its Young* (1972). In 1974 Hazel was convicted on drug and assault charges; the band replaced him temporarily and he returned to an again-reduced role. In 1977 Hazel recorded a solo album, *Game, Dames And Guitar Thangs*, which featured members of Parliament-Funkadelic. Hazel died in 1992 after a long struggle with stomach problems. Three collections of his unreleased recordings included the 1994 four-song EP 'Jams From The Heart', 2000's *Rest in P* and 2006's *Eddie Hazel At Home*.

### DATE OF BIRTH/DEATH

10 April 1950/23 December 1992

### PLACE OF BIRTH

New York, USA

### GENRES

Funk

# JIMI HENDRIX
## THE GUITAR EXPERIENCE

Jimi Hendrix was born in Seattle in 1942 but there was no hint of his future success before he moved to England in 1966. There Hendrix formed The Jimi Hendrix Experience with bassist Noel Redding and drummer Mitch Mitchell. He recorded a version of 'Hey Joe', creating a buzz that launched his career. *Are You Experienced* (1967) was an audacious debut album, opening up a new world of guitar sounds. *Axis: Bold As Love* (1967) pushed the sonic innovations and was an instant hit. *Electric Ladyland* (1968) was his most ambitious and successful record, a double album that ranged from the futuristic funk of 'Crosstown Traffic' to the emblematic style of 'Voodoo Child (Slight Return)'.

Tensions in the band resulted in its dissolution in 1969, and Hendrix formed Gypsy Sun And Rainbow, who made a tentative debut at the Woodstock Festival in August. Within a month the band had disintegrated and Hendrix re-emerged with a new trio called the Band Of Gypsys. *Band Of Gypsys* (1970) was the last Hendrix album released before he died of an overdose of sleeping tablets. In the aftermath of his death, unreleased studio recordings were hurriedly released, bearing no relation to the album that he had nearly completed at the time of his death. It wasn't until 1997 that *First Rays Of The New Rising Sun* was released, while his last recordings with The Experience came out in 2010 as *Valleys of Neptune*.

### DATE OF BIRTH/DEATH

27 November 1942/18 September 1970

### PLACE OF BIRTH

Seattle, USA

### GENRES

Rock

# ALLAN HOLDSWORTH

## THE MYSTIFYING MASTER

Of all the guitar players of the last 40 years, none produce music as confounding yet beautiful as Allan Holdsworth. He was influenced early on by the electric–guitar playing of jazz pioneer Charlie Christian and saxophonist John Coltrane, whose 'sheets of sound' approach had a profound effect on the guitarist. Holdsworth's first professional recording came in 1969, with a mildly psychedelic jazz–pop outing titled *'Igginbottom's Wrench*, on which Holdsworth was already developing his signature phrasing and improvisational tools. He then spent time in Tempest, before returning to the fusion of Soft Machine, Tony Williams' Lifetime, Jean–Luc Ponty and the progressive–rock supergroup UK.

By the late Seventies, Holdsworth decided to pursue a solo career, and released *I.O.U.* (1982) and *Road Games* (1983). Up to that point, Holdsworth had primarily used Fender Strats, Gibson SGs and Charvel 'super–strats'. But after he released *Metal Fatigue* in 1985, Holdsworth discovered the SynthAxe MIDI guitar controller and he soon took guitar synthesis to new and exciting musical realms. After nearly 20 solo albums and a five–year hiatus from the music industry, Holdsworth re-emerged as a touring artist in 2006, just in time for a whole new generation of guitarists to ponder his otherworldly fretboard abilities.

**DATE OF BIRTH**

6 August 1946

**PLACE OF BIRTH**

Bradford, England

**GENRES**

Jazz, Rock, Pop, Progressive Rock

# BUDDY HOLLY

## STRUMMING SAViOUR

Buddy Holly helped define and popularize rock'n'roll in its earliest days. Strumming a Fender Stratocaster, he brought an extra dose of country to a sound that was still closely related to pure blues and R&B. Holly originally sang in a bluegrass duo, but turned to rock after seeing Elvis Presley sing live in early 1955. Signing with Decca Records, he cut an early version of 'That'll Be The Day', which secured his success, and followed it with a string of hits such as 'Everyday', 'Peggy Sue', 'Maybe Baby' and 'Rave On'. With his new band The Crickets he won over the crowd at Harlem's Apollo Theater and toured the UK in 1958.

The Crickets left Holly as he became a national figure, and he toured with a new backup band. On a tour with Ritchie Valens and the Big Bopper, Holly chartered a plane to fly him from a performance in Clear Lake, Iowa, to Fargo, North Dakota, in February 1959. The plane crashed, killing the three young stars. The prolific Holly had recorded so many songs that 'new' records were released for the next 10 years, influencing a generation of songwriters and inspiring legions to take up guitar.

### DATE OF BIRTH/DEATH

7 September 1936/3 February 1959

### PLACE OF BIRTH

Lubbock, USA

### GENRES

Rock'n'Roll, Rockabilly

# JOHN LEE HOOKER

## THE BOOGIE MAN

The original boogie man, John Lee Hooker sustained a career of more than 50 years with his incessant one–chord stomp and half–spoken vocal style. He made his first recordings in Detroit in 1948, including 'Boogie Chillen', which was a No. 1 R&B hit. Hooker immediately cashed in, recording further hits such as 'Hobo Blues' (1948), 'Crawling Kingsnake' (1949) and 'I'm In The Mood' (1951). In the mid–Fifties Hooker started recording with an electric band, heightening his rhythmic emphasis with songs such as 'Dimples' and 'Boom Boom'. At the same time, he enjoyed a parallel career as a solo folk/blues artist, although by the end of the decade he was back in the rock fold, thanks to the success of his disciples Canned Heat, who repaid their debt by recruiting him for *Hooker 'N Heat* (1970).

Further collaborations with Van Morrison and guitarist Elvin Bishop maintained Hooker's profile in the Seventies, but his career sagged in the Eighties before a sudden revival in 1989 with *The Healer*. The album's success set Hooker up for the Nineties as Van Morrison and Keith Richards, among others, queued up to appear on subsequent albums, including *The Hook* (1990), *Mr Lucky* (1991), and *Boom Boom* (1992). Hooker died in 2001 at the age of 83.

### DATE OF BIRTH/DEATH

22 August 1917/21 June 2001

### PLACE OF BIRTH

Clarksdale, USA

### GENRES

Blues, R&B, Folk, Rock

# STEVE HOWE

## THE YES MAN

Steve Howe played with Tomorrow and Bodast before he joined Yes in 1970. They were redefining their style for their third album, *The Yes Album* (1971), and Howe made an immediate impact with his jangling, jazzy/country playing. *Fragile* (1972) brought together the classic Yes line-up – Howe, Rick Wakeman, Chris Squire, Jon Anderson and Bill Bruford – and marked the band's commercial breakthrough. *Yessongs* (1973) demonstrated their live prowess, with Howe revealing himself as more of a rock guitarist than he had in the studio. After several changes to the line-up the band lost cohesion and split in 1981.

Howe then formed Asia, whose self-titled debut became a worldwide hit. After *Alpha* (1983), however, Howe left the band and formed the short-lived GTR. There followed various Yes reunions, resulting in the albums *Anderson Bruford Wakeman Howe* (1989) and *Union* (1991), after which Howe went solo again (he had released two solo albums in the Seventies), releasing *Turbulence* (1991), *The Grand Scheme Of Things* (1993), *Not Necessarily Acoustic* (1994) and *Homebrew* (1996). In 1995 a reunited Yes produced a live album, *Keys To Ascension* (1996). Howe has contributed to every Yes album since then, while participating in Asia reunions and maintaining his solo career.

### DATE OF BIRTH

8 April 1947

### PLACE OF BIRTH

London, England

### GENRES

Progressive Rock, Hard Rock, Pop, Jazz

# TONY IOMMI

## BLACK SABBATH'S IRON MAN

In 1967, after playing in various local acts, Tony Iommi (pictured left) hooked up with three former schoolmates – Bill Ward (drums), Terry 'Geezer' Butler (bass) and John 'Ozzy' Osbourne (vocals, pictured right) – to form the blues-rock outfit Earth. An accident at the sheet–metal factory where he worked left Iommi without the tips of two of his fingers, but the disciplined young guitarist persevered. With the band's name change to Black Sabbath, a darker and heavier musical direction emerged. Originally a dedicated Fender Stratocaster player, on recording their self–titled debut one of Iommi's pickups blew, so he picked up a Gibson SG and his iconic sound. When Sabbath released their landmark album *Paranoid* in 1971, it was clear that heavy metal was here to stay, and the band's next three albums, *Master Of Reality* (1971), *Vol. 4* (1972) and *Sabbath Bloody Sabbath* (1973), made them the most influential heavy metal band of all time.

After Osbourne's departure in 1979, Iommi kept Sabbath going with a rotating stable of singers. In 1998, the original line–up released *Reunion*, a live album that earned them a second chance in the spotlight. They headlined several festivals in the Noughties, inspiring an enthusiastic new generation of metal fans and musicians. Iommi continues to tour and record with Osbourne replacement Ronnie James Dio in the band Heaven & Hell.

**DATE OF BIRTH**

19 February 1948

**PLACE OF BIRTH**

Birmingham, England

**GENRES**

Heavy Metal, Rock, Blues Rock

A–Z OF
GUITAR GODS

# ELMORE JAMES

## THE BOTTLENECK ELECTRIFIED

The swooping, full-octave slide-guitar riff that opened Elmore James's first record, 'Dust My Broom' (1951), established one of the basic riffs of post-war blues. Bottleneck guitar had always been part of the blues, but James was the first to use it in a hard-rocking electric-blues context. He cut several versions, recording a new one every time he switched record labels – which was often. Many of his other songs were close copies, including 'Dust My Blues', 'I Believe' and 'Wild About You Baby'. But James was no one-trick pony. His version of Tampa Red's 'It Hurts Me Too' and his own interchangeable 'The Sun Is Shining' and 'The Sky Is Crying' each have an impressive, slow-burning intensity.

James hung out with Sonny Boy Williamson II and Robert Johnson in his teens. He played regularly with Williamson and in 1952 he moved to Chicago, where his primal riffs were an instant success. He formed The Broomdusters and soon became a popular attraction on the live scene. His final recordings were made in New Orleans in 1961, featuring the frisky 'Look On Yonder Wall' and 'Shake Your Moneymaker'. James later died of a heart attack at the age of 45.

**DATE OF BIRTH/DEATH**

27 January 1918/24 May 1963

**PLACE OF BIRTH**

Richland, USA

**GENRES**

Blues, Electric Blues

# BERT JANSCH

## PENTANGLE'S FOLK HERO

Bert Jansch acquired a guitar as a teenager and started visiting a local folk club, where he was introduced to the music of Big Bill Broonzy, Pete Seeger and others. He became a full–time musician and spent two years playing one–night stands in British folk clubs. He recorded *Bert Jansch* in 1965, which included his protest song 'Do You Hear Me Now'. *Jack Orion* (1966) contained his first recording of 'Blackwaterside', recorded by Led Zeppelin as 'Black Mountain Side'.

Jansch and John Renbourn frequently played together, and in 1966 they recorded *Bert And John*. In 1967, the duo formed the group Pentangle with singer Jacqui McShee, Danny Thompson (string bass) and Terry Cox (drums). Pentangle's first album was released in 1968. The group toured extensively, playing many of Jansch's original compositions. Jansch continued to record as a solo act, releasing *Rosemary Lane* in 1971. Pentangle split in 1973, and Jansch withdrew temporarily from the concert circuit. He returned in 1977 with a new group and the album *A Rare Conundrum*. Jansch's 1979 album, *Avocet*, was one of his most ambitious. His subsequent albums, including *The Black Swan* (2006), have kept his fans loyal, and he has toured the world and performed regularly in London venues.

**DATE OF BIRTH**

3 November 1943

**PLACE OF BIRTH**

Glasgow, Scotland

**GENRES**

Folk

# BLIND LEMON JEFFERSON

## A COUNTRY BLUESMAN

Blind Lemon Jefferson played country blues, a style he customized by listening to the flamenco intonations of local Mexican guitarists in his native Texas, as well as cotton-field songs. He developed a fast, complex guitar technique that has never been duplicated, although his lyrics have been widely appropriated by other performers for their own songs.

Little is known about Jefferson before 1926. He was reportedly born blind (although the only known photograph shows him wearing glasses), in 1893 or 1894. He played house parties, brothels and drinking dens in his late teens and was eventually contacted by Paramount Records, who recorded him in Chicago. There he opened up the market for blues records when 'Got The Blues' became the biggest-selling record by a black male artist. Songs such as 'Black Snake Moan' had a blatant sexual theme, and cheating women were a concern on 'Eagle Eyed Mama', but the likes of 'One Dime Blues', 'Prison Cell Blues' and 'See That My Grave Is Kept Clean' hint at deeper fears. Confusion surrounds Jefferson's death in Chicago in 1929. It was said that he froze to death, but a heart attack in the back of his car seems more likely.

### DATE OF BIRTH/DEATH

24 September 1893 or 26 October 1894/12 December 1929

### PLACE OF BIRTH

Coutchman, USA

### GENRES

Country Blues

# JOHN 5

## THE MODERN-DAY HERO

John 5 (born John Lowery) started playing guitar at the age of seven. When he turned 18, he moved to California to pursue a career as a professional session guitarist. There he met producer Bob Marlette and began working on a number of TV shows, commercials and film soundtracks. After touring with Lita Ford and k.d. lang, and working on short-lived projects with drummer Randy Castillo and singer Rob Halford, John landed a gig with David Lee Roth's DLR Band. Shortly thereafter, shock-rocker Marilyn Manson hired him, giving him his current moniker. John 5 played with Manson until April 2004, when he set out to record his first solo album, *Vertigo* (2004).

With *Vertigo* and *Songs For Sanity* (2005), John 5 revealed to his primarily metal fan base a multifaceted approach to guitar that includes heavy bluegrass and country influences. That unusual musical pedigree created an underground buzz in the guitar community. Since then, a permanent gig with metal superstar Rob Zombie, and the 2007 release of the instrumental *The Devil Knows My Name*, has garnered John 5 even greater appeal. In 2008, *Guitar Edge* magazine proclaimed him one of the 'new guitar heroes'. Finally, it seems, John 5 is getting some time in the spotlight. His 2010 album, *The Art Of Malice*, is due for release on 11 May.

### DATE OF BIRTH

31 July 1971

### PLACE OF BIRTH

Grosse Pointe, USA

### GENRES

Heavy Metal, Hard Rock Bluegrass, Shred

# ERIC JOHNSON

## INSTRUMENTAL IDEAL

Encouraged by his parents, Eric Johnson started playing guitar at the age of 11. He formed a fusion band, The Electromagnetics, building a reputation around Texas in the mid–Seventies, but his career was effectively buried when he signed a six–year contract with a production company that failed to release his album, *Seven Worlds*, recorded in 1977. Johnson resumed his career in 1984, signing to Warner Brothers and releasing his first album, *Tones* (1986). Despite critical praise, the album did not sell well. He spent four years recording his next album, *Ah Via Musicom* (1990), and this time the sales matched the reviews. However, it was another six years before he released *Venus Isle* (1996), featuring more rock instrumentals ('Camel's Night Out', 'Pavilion'), blues ('SRV') and jazz ('Manhattan'). In 1996 he was part of the first G3 guitarists tour of North America with Joe Satriani and Steve Vai.

Johnson's obsessive quest for perfection has restricted his career, although it has enhanced his cult status. *Live & Beyond* (2000), recorded with power trio Alien Love Child, was a blues–oriented album. *Bloom* (2005) was a reflection of his continually nomadic musical styles. Johnson mostly plays a Stratocaster, although he also plays vintage Gibson guitars and a Flying V.

**DATE OF BIRTH**

17 August 1954

**PLACE OF BIRTH**

Austin, USA

**GENRES**

Hard Rock, Instrumental Rock

# ROBERT JOHNSON

## BLUES MYTH MAKER

Robert Johnson's influence on the blues is out of all proportion to his career and output – he died relatively unknown at the age of 27 and recorded just 29 songs. The legend was fostered by the Sixties generation of British blues guitarists, led by Eric Clapton and Keith Richards, who were in thrall to *King Of The Delta Blues Singers* (1962), a collection of Johnson's songs that personified the iconic image of a blues singer.

In fact the myths had started before Johnson even made a record. As a teenager he hung around with Charley Patton, Son House and Willie Brown. He disappeared for two years and, when he returned, the dramatic improvement in his playing led to speculation that Johnson had sold his soul to the devil. Songs such as 'Preaching Blues (Up Jumped The Devil)', 'Hellhound On My Trail' and 'Me And The Devil Blues' did nothing to dispel those notions. Johnson recorded twice, in 1936 and 1937, and released 11 records, the most popular of which was the bawdy 'Terraplane Blues'. While his ardent disciples have left some of his most haunting songs alone, others such as 'I Believe I'll Dust My Broom', 'Come On In My Kitchen' and 'Walking Blues' have become part of the standard blues repertoire.

### DATE OF BIRTH/DEATH

8 May 1911/16 August 1938

### PLACE OF BIRTH

Hazlehurst, USA

### GENRES

Delta Blues, Country Blues

# DAVEY JOHNSTONE
## VERSATILITY AND COMMAND

Davey Johnstone rocketed to fame with the Rocket Man himself, Elton John, as the former Reg Dwight exploded on the music scene in the early Seventies. Except for a short period from the late Seventies to early Eighties, Johnstone has always occupied the nucleus of John's band.

Johnstone was a busy studio acoustic guitarist when he was asked to join the British folk group Magna Carta. He recorded three albums with them, playing a variety of instruments including guitar, mandolin, sitar and dulcimer. Producer Gus Dudgeon asked Johnstone to play on a self-titled 1970 solo album by a new artist, Bernie Taupin. Taupin's collaborator, John, then invited Johnstone to play on *Madman Across The Water* (1971). Johnstone found a niche for himself on the prolific John's piano-based arrangements, ranging from *Madman*'s moody atmospherics to his signature crunch on 'Saturday Night's Alright For Fighting'. He has occasionally worked with other acts, including future wife Kiki Dee, Joan Armatrading, The Who, Bob Seger, Rod Stewart and Vonda Shepherd. He also released a solo album, *Smiling Face* (1973), and an album of acoustic instrumentation, *Crop Circles* (1998). In 1996, Johnstone released a video of instructional guitar, on which he plays a wide variety of Elton John classics.

### DATE OF BIRTH
6 May 1951

### PLACE OF BIRTH
Edinburgh, Scotland

### GENRES
Rock, Pop

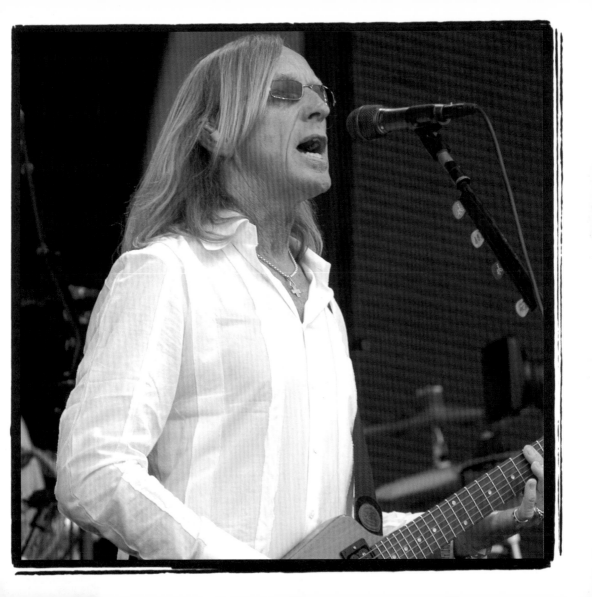

# ADAM JONES

## ALTERNATIVE ALL THE WAY

Alternative–metal guitarist Adam Jones formed Tool in 1990 with Danny Carey (drums), Maynard James Keenan (vocals) and Paul D'Amour (bass). The band's recorded debut, the EP 'Opiate' (1992), was firmly in heavy–metal mode, but *Undertow* (1993), *Ænima* (1996), *Lateralus* (2001) and *10,000 Days* (2006) took the band in less easily classifiable directions that have been described as art rock, alternative metal, progressive metal and psychedelic metal. The use of unpredictable time signatures, of which 'Schism' from *Lateralus* is a prime example, and their commitment to experimentation have resulted in Tool being hailed as standard bearers for the new prog rock.

Jones employs a multiplicity of techniques: power chords, arpeggios, offbeat rhythms and minimalism. On 'Jambi', from *10,000 Days*, he played the solo on a talk box. Although wary of the overuse of effects, he has employed several, in particular the wah–wah, plus a flanger, digital delay and volume pedal. He uses an electric hair remover for women's legs in preference to an E–bow, claiming that it produces a better sound. He favours Gibson Silverburst Les Paul Customs made between 1978 and 1985 and owns five. He has also used a Gibson SG and is rumoured to have played a Fender Telecaster on *10,000 Days*. Tool toured in 2009 and are rumoured to be currently recording a new album.

### DATE OF BIRTH

15 January 1965

### PLACE OF BIRTH

Park Ridge, USA

### GENRES

Alternative Metal, Progressive Rock

# STANLEY JORDAN

## THE TWO-HANDED TAPPER

Stanley Jordan caught listeners' attention with his touch technique, an advanced form of two-handed tapping. By quickly tapping his finger down behind the appropriate fret with varying force, Jordan produced a unique legato sound not usually associated with tapping. He was the first artist to be signed by the relaunched Blue Note Records in 1985 and *Magic Touch* (1985) was the label's first new release. Smooth-jazz radio embraced his versions of 'The Lady In My Life' and The Beatles' 'Eleanor Rigby', helping *Magic Touch* top *Billboard*'s jazz chart for 51 weeks.

Subsequent albums included a solo-guitar project titled *Standards Volume 1* (1986), on which Jordan rightfully assigned the category to pop songs by Stevie Wonder and Simon & Garfunkel as well as standards by Henry Mancini ('Moon River') and Hoagy Carmichael ('Georgia On My Mind'). *Flying Home* (1988) and *Cornucopia* (1990) followed. A move to Arista Records resulted in *Bolero*, which featured a 17-minute arrangement of Ravel's 'Bolero' broken up into multiple stylistic sections. Jordan eventually left the mainstream record business. He now owns a book and music store, and studies music therapy, although he continues to tour.

**DATE OF BIRTH**

31 July 1959

**PLACE OF BIRTH**

Chicago, USA

**GENRES**

Jazz, Fusion

# ALBERT KING

## GOT BLUES AND SOUL

At six feet four inches tall Albert King cut an imposing figure on stage. Equally distinctive was his Gibson Flying V guitar, a right-handed instrument that King played left-handed and upside down, giving him an unusual, tormented sound. His career was a slow burner: he didn't release a record, 'Be On Your Merry Way', until 1953, and it wasn't until 1964 that he scored a minor hit with 'Don't Throw Your Love On Me So Strong'. His fortunes changed when he signed to Stax in 1966 and was paired with Booker T & The MGs. Their first session produced 'Laundromat Blues', which put the blues into a modern context. *Born Under A Bad Sign* (1967) was acclaimed as one of the most stirring blues albums of the era.

King was the first blues artist to play San Francisco's famed Fillmore, and the resulting album, *Live Wire/Blues Power* (1968), was a template for a new generation of blues bands in the American South. In the Seventies King added funk to his bluesy soul on *I'll Play The Blues For You* (1973). He planned to retire in the late Eighties, but died of a heart attack in 1992, just two days after another farewell performance.

### DATE OF BIRTH/DEATH

25 April 1923/21 December 1992

### PLACE OF BIRTH

Indianola, USA

### GENRES

Blues, R&B, Electric Blues, Soul

# B.B. KING

## BLUES AMBASSADOR

Born in Mississippi (his style draws on that of Mississippi bluesmen Elmore James and Muddy Waters, among others), King found his voice in a gospel choir. He moved to Memphis in his early twenties, securing a sponsored radio spot. King scored a No. 1 R&B record with 'Three O'Clock Blues' (1952) and followed it with a string of hits: 'You Know I Love You' (1952), Please Love Me' (1953), 'You Upset Me Baby' (1954), 'Sweet Little Angel' (1956) and 'Sweet Sixteen' (1960). In the Sixties, King signed to MCA to broaden his audience. *Live At The Regal* (1964) failed in that respect, but later in the Sixties he found an appreciative audience in the rock scene, scoring a Top 20 hit with 'The Thrill Is Gone' (1970).

Through the Seventies King regularly toured Europe, taking on the ambassadorial role that enabled him to survive passing fashions and occasionally hitting the spotlight – such as his collaboration with U2 in 1988 on 'When Love Comes To Town'. In 2006 he undertook a farewell world tour but he was still making appearances in 2008. King's constant companion since 1950 has been Lucille, originally a Gibson ES–335 but for the past 25 years a solid–body Gibson ES–355.

### DATE OF BIRTH

16 September 1925

### PLACE OF BIRTH

Itta Bena, USA

### GENRES

Memphis Blues, R&B, Soul Blues

A-Z OF
GUITAR GODS

# FREDDIE KING

## BRINGING BLUES TO ROCK

Freddie King revitalized the Chicago blues scene in the Sixties and helped set up the blues–rock movement. Born in Texas, King moved to Chicago in 1950 and immersed himself in the thriving blues scene. From guitarist Jimmy Rogers he learnt a thumb–and–index–finger picking technique that he modified by using a plastic thumb pick and a steel fingerpick that added to his keening technique.

But it was hard to get a break in a blues scene dominated by Muddy Waters and Howlin' Wolf. When he finally landed a record deal in 1960 he had a stack of material ready, and at his first session he cut 'Have You Ever Loved A Woman' and the instrumental 'Hideaway', which was a Top 5 R&B hit in 1961 and even made the pop Top 30. An album of snazzy instrumentals, *Let's Hide Away And Dance Away With Freddy King* (1961), and *Freddy King Gives You A Bonanza Of Instrumentals* (1965) followed. Although the hits dried up by the mid–Sixties, his guitar prowess continued to develop and he remained a top live attraction on both sides of the Atlantic until his fatal heart attack at the age of 42.

### DATE OF BIRTH/DEATH

3 September 1934/28 December 1976

### PLACE OF BIRTH

Gilmer, USA

### GENRES

Blues, R&B

# MARK KNOPFLER

## DIRE STRAITS TO MASTER

From the unlikeliest of beginnings in the British new wave of the late Seventies, Dire Straits became one of the biggest bands of the Eighties, due in large part to Mark Knopfler's unassuming but compelling finger-picking guitar style. The band formed in 1977 and secured a contract with Vertigo Records after sending a demo tape of 'Sultans Of Swing' to DJ Charlie Gillett. *Dire Straits* (1978) attracted little attention in Britain but took off in Europe and then America, where 'Sultans Of Swing' was a No. 2 hit. *Communiqué* (1979) maintained the stripped-down sound, while *Making Movies* (1980) and *Love Over Gold* (1982) stretched out their country-rock groove. But it was 1985's *Brothers In Arms* that captured the zeitgeist, becoming the first-ever million-selling CD. Afterwards Knopfler switched to solo projects, including soundtracks and forming the low-key country outfit Notting Hillbillies.

Dire Straits reformed for *On Every Street* (1991) and played another world tour that produced a live album, *On The Night* (1993), before Knopfler dissolved the band for good and continued to pursue a solo career that has included *Golden Heart* (1996), *Sailing To Philadelphia* (2000), *The Ragpicker's Dream* (2002) and *Shangri-La* (2006), while producing and recording albums with the likes of Emmylou Harris (*All The Roadrunning*, 2006). Although Knopfler is left-handed, he plays right-handed guitars, usually Fender Stratocasters and Telecasters.

### DATE OF BIRTH

12 August 1949

### PLACE OF BIRTH

Glasgow, Scotland

### GENRES

Rock, Country, Blues

# PAUL KOSSOFF

## FREE FOR ALL

Paul Kossoff began his career in R&B band Black Cat Bones in 1966. The band often supported Fleetwood Mac, and a friendship arose between Peter Green and Kossoff, based on their shared enthusiasm for the blues. Kossoff saw Paul Rodgers singing in Brown Sugar, which led to the formation of Free at the height of the British blues boom in 1968. Bassist Andy Fraser was recruited at the suggestion of pioneering blues musician Alexis Korner, who also came up with the band's name.

Free's debut *Tons Of Sobs* (1969) showcased the band's blues rock at its rawest, driven by Kossoff's guitar. 'Goin' Down Slow' featured his long, complex solo. Before *Fire And Water* (1970), Kossoff was disillusioned by the band's lack of commercial success until the classic single 'All Right Now' rectified that. Kossoff's aggressive riff, played on his trademark Gibson Les Paul, remains his best-known work. Free temporarily split after the failure of *Highway* (1971) but reconvened for *Free At Last* (1972). Kossoff's drug problems led him to distance himself from the band, but he completed a solo album, *Back Street Crawler* (1973), and assembled a band of the same name, which made two albums. He suffered a drug-induced heart attack on a plane in 1976.

### DATE OF BIRTH/DEATH

14 September 1950/19 March 1976

### PLACE OF BIRTH

London, England

### GENRES

Rock, Hard Rock, Blues Rock

A-Z OF
GUITAR GODS

# LENNY KRAVITZ

## RETRO ROCKER AND TRENDSETTER

Producer-performer Lenny Kravitz has explored multiple genres during his 25-year career as a music star, but has often been thought of as married to retro styles. He decided to pursue rock'n'roll while in high school and at first patterned his style and approach after Prince. Later he began looking to classic rockers for inspiration. He issued his debut, *Let Love Rule*, in 1989; the title track was a hit and Kravitz gained a reputation as a trendsetter. He began to compose for other artists, writing Madonna's 'Justify My Love'.

Kravitz's work in the Nineties included: *Mama Said* (1992), which included the funk rocker 'Always On The Run' and the soul ballad 'It Ain't Over 'Til It's Over'; 1993's *Are You Gonna Go My Way*, which made Kravitz an arena headliner and media star; and 1998's *5*, which included the biggest hit of his career, 'Fly Away', and the hit remake of The Guess Who's 'American Woman'. In the twenty-first century, Kravitz continued to record and branched out with a design company. He recorded a funky version of John Lennon's 'Cold Turkey' for Amnesty International's 2007 benefit compilation *Instant Karma*. Kravitz returned in 2008 with *It Is Time For A Love Revolution*. Its follow-up, *Negrophilia*, is due for release in 2010.

### DATE OF BIRTH

26 May 1964

### PLACE OF BIRTH

New York, USA

### GENRES

Rock, Pop, Funk Rock, R&B

# ROBBY KRIEGER

## OPENING DOORS

Eclectic guitarist Robby Krieger started to play the blues on piano and began to learn guitar at the age of 17. While playing in The Psychedelic Rangers, he and drummer John Densmore hooked up with keyboardist Ray Manzarek and singer Jim Morrison to form The Doors. Their debut album *The Doors* (1967) was an instant sensation and 'Light My Fire' became a massive Summer of Love hit in America. Krieger's discordant solo on 'When the Music's Over' from *Strange Days* (1967) anticipated Robert Fripp's style, while his vibrato on the introduction to 'Riders on the Storm' from *LA Woman* (1971) evoked gentle rainfall. He generally favoured a Gibson SG, although he has also used a Les Paul Sunburst and a Fender Stratocaster.

The Doors made two albums after Morrison's death and later reunited for *An American Prayer* (1978), adding music to tapes of Morrison reading his poetry. Krieger has also made several jazz-tinged solo albums. The Doors' enduring popularity inspired Krieger and Manzarek to assemble a new version of the band in 2002 with former Cult singer Ian Astbury but without Densmore, who subsequently took legal action to prevent the use of The Doors' name. The move forced the outfit to tour as Riders On The Storm.

**DATE OF BIRTH**

8 January 1946

**PLACE OF BIRTH**

Los Angeles, USA

**GENRES**

Rock, Blues

# SONNY LANDRETH

## LOUISIANA LEGEND

Sonny Landreth became immersed in Louisiana's swamp–pop and Zydeco music as a child and was a guitar virtuoso by his teens. His first professional appearance was with Clifton Chenier, in whose Red Hot Louisiana Band Landreth was the only white musician. He recorded two albums for the Louisiana independent Blues Unlimited label, *Blues Attack* (1981) and *Way Down* (1985), the second of which came to the attention of record companies in Nashville. This led to Landreth recording and touring with John Hiatt, after which he was offered more session work with a range of musicians, notably John Mayall, who recorded Landreth's song 'Congo Square'. He resumed his solo career with *Outward Bound* (1992), and continues to play live.

Landreth's unique style of playing has left many guitarists puzzling over how he achieves the powerful and sweet sound from his trademark National guitar. Landreth's strings are positioned high off the frets, allowing him to play notes, chords and chord fragments behind the slide, which is placed on his little finger. His right–hand technique is highly distinctive, involving slapping, tapping and picking the strings with his fingers. He also employs numerous different tunings – so many that he has developed an automatic tuner that is mounted on the guitar.

**DATE OF BIRTH**

1 February 1951

**PLACE OF BIRTH**

Canton, USA

**GENRES**

Blues

# ALBERT LEE

## TRIUMPH ON A TELECASTER

Rock guitarist Albert Lee started his musical career on piano but, like many of his generation, took up guitar upon the arrival of rock'n'roll. He played in various bands, before becoming lead guitarist with Chris Farlowe & The Thunderbirds. Preferring country to the soul-influenced music of Farlowe, he left in 1968 to join country-rock outfit Head, Hands & Feet, with whom he made his name. In 1974, Lee relocated to Los Angeles, where he found himself in demand as a session musician but unable to progress his solo career. He joined Emmylou Harris's Hot Band in 1976 and, two years later, he linked up with Eric Clapton, with whom he played for the next five years. In 1987, Lee fronted a band for the first time, Hogan's Heroes, with whom he still tours regularly and released *Like This* in 2008.

Because of his long association with the Fender instrument, Lee has become known as 'Mr Telecaster', although he has also played Gibson guitars, an Ernie Ball Music Man and a Stratocaster from time to time. Lee has not been rewarded with great commercial success or fame but is widely admired by his peers, renowned for his finger-style and hybrid picking techniques.

**DATE OF BIRTH**

21 December 1943

**PLACE OF BIRTH**

Leominster, England

**GENRES**

Rock, Country Rock

# ALVIN LEE

## TITAN OF TEN YEARS AFTER

Inspired by rock'n'roll guitarists Chuck Berry and Scotty Moore, Alvin Lee formed his first band, Ivan Jay & the Jaymen, in 1960. They moved to London in 1966 and changed their name to Ten Years After. Debut album *Ten Years After* (1967) showcased Lee's soulful, nimble–fingered guitar playing and the band's trailblazing mix of swing jazz, blues and rock. An appearance at the Woodstock Festival in 1969 provided their breakthrough in the States. The band also played the Isle of Wight Festival in 1970, the year of their only British hit single, 'Love Like A Man'. After nine studio albums, Lee disbanded Ten Years After in 1974.

His career outside the band had already begun with *On The Road To Freedom* (1973), a country–rock collaboration with Mylon LeFevre that boasted George Harrison, Ronnie Wood and Steve Winwood amongst its superstar guests. In 1978, he put together a new version of Ten Years After, and he toured under the name again in 1989. In the Nineties, he recorded with rock'n'roll pioneers Scotty Moore and D.J. Fontana. Lee's favourite guitar is his long–serving Gibson Custom Shop 335, affectionately dubbed 'Big Red'. As it is too valuable to take on the road, the company made him a copy of it. His last album, *Saguitar*, was released in 2007.

**DATE OF BIRTH**

19 December 1944

**PLACE OF BIRTH**

Nottingham, England

**GENRES**

Rock, Blues Rock, Country Rock

# JAKE E. LEE

## OZZY TO BADLANDS TO LEGEND

Jakey Lou Williams 'Jake E. Lee' (pictured right) formed a band called Teaser in high school, and they went on to dominate the San Diego club scene. He next joined Stephen Pearcy's band Mickey Rat, which moved to Los Angeles and changed its name to Ratt. After developing a huge following on the LA scene, Lee decided to leave the band. After a few gigs with Rough Cutt, Lee was chosen by Ozzy Osbourne (pictured right) to fill the vacancy left by the death of lead guitarist Randy Rhoads. Lee's playing shone bright on 1983's *Bark At The Moon*, particularly on the title track. *The Ultimate Sin* (1986) followed and peaked at No. 1 on the album charts. Despite the album's success, Osbourne fired Lee in the midst of one of his frequent rages.

Lee hooked up with ex–Black Sabbath singer Ray Gillen in 1989 to form the blues–metal outfit Badlands. Their self-titled debut received critical acclaim but weak public support. Their follow-up, *Voodoo Highway* (1991), represented an even deeper journey into the blues and again earned critical raves. Since Badlands, Lee has been invited to play on several compilation and tribute albums. He also released a solo album called *A Fine Pink Mist* in 1996, and recorded an album of blues covers, *Retraced* (2005).

**DATE OF BIRTH**

15 February 1957

**PLACE OF BIRTH**

Norfolk, USA

**GENRES**

Hard Rock, Heavy Metal, Blues

# ALEX LIFESON
## RUSH TO ROCK LEGEND

Alex Lifeson formed his first substantive band in 1968, teaming with drummer John Rutsey and bassist Geddy Lee and calling themselves Rush. After several years on the Toronto covers circuit, the trio signed a deal with Mercury Records and released their self–titled debut in 1974. Soon after, Rutsey left the group, opening the door for virtuoso drummer Neil Peart. After two more albums in 1975, *Fly By Night* and *Caress Of Steel*, the trio broke through in 1976 with *2112*, an album of epic, complex tunes that carried the band to the top of the progressive–rock mountain. The band's next three albums – *A Farewell To Kings* (1977), *Hemispheres* (1978) and *Permanent Waves* (1980) – burnished the trio's reputation as superior instrumentalists, while songs such as 'Closer to the Heart', 'Xanadu', 'La Villa Strangiato', 'Free Will' and 'The Spirit Of Radio' established Lifeson as a bona fide guitar hero. In 1981 Rush achieved its greatest commercial success with the release of *Moving Pictures*, featuring the cult hit 'Tom Sawyer'.

During the Eighties Rush experimented heavily with synthesizers, crafting a more futuristic sound, but by 1993's *Counterparts* the band had largely gone back to guitar– and riff–driven songwriting; their 2007 release, *Snakes And Arrows*, contained no keyboards whatsoever and saw them tour into 2008.

**DATE OF BIRTH**

27 August 1953

**PLACE OF BIRTH**

Fernie, Canada

**GENRES**

Hard Rock, Progressive Rock, Heavy Metal

# STEVE LUKATHER

## TOTO TO THRILLING LICKS

Lukather met Jeff and Steve Porcaro and David Paich in high school. All were becoming active in the burgeoning LA studio scene, and The Porcaro brothers were crucial to Lukather's obtaining session work and burnishing his reputation as a multi-style studio guitarist. By the time he was asked to join The Porcaros, Paich, David Hungate and singer Bobby Kimball in Toto, Lukather had already recorded and toured with Boz Skaggs. He later played on hundreds of hit records, including releases by Leo Sayer, Boz Scaggs, Alice Cooper, Barbra Streisand, The Pointer Sisters, Cher and Cheap Trick.

Toto garnered a lot of buzz with their debut album and exploded two years later with *Toto IV* (1982). After that the band settled into a long run with a mostly international cult following, but Lukather's reputation grew. Beginning with breakout performances on Michael Jackson's *Thriller* (1982), he became a superstar guitarist and took on a larger role with Toto, co-writing the majority of the group's songs and taking over lead vocals until he left the group and they split in 2008. Lukather had already launched a solo career in the late Eighties and won a Grammy for 2001's *No Substitutions*. Lukather plays his own MusicMan signature model 'Luke', which incorporates his signature EMG pickup system.

**DATE OF BIRTH**

21 October 1957

**PLACE OF BIRTH**

San Fernando Valley, USA

**GENRES**

Hard Rock, Progressive Rock, Pop Rock, Jazz Fusion

A–Z OF
GUITAR GODS

# YNGWIE MALMSTEEN

## A GUITAR FORCE

A leading figure of Eighties 'neo-classical' rock guitarists, Yngwie Malmsteen learned his breakneck arpeggios and baroque composing style from classical composers and performers as well as rock artists. His own sweep-picking technique, use of harmonic scales and pedal tones and aggressive playing have helped create his unique style.

A demo tape that Malmsteen unsuccessfully sent around to Swedish record companies was picked up by US label Shrapnel, and he was invited to join metal band Steeler. He played on their self-titled debut album (1983) before moving on to Alcatrazz, where he had more input, recording *No Parole For Rock & Roll* (1984) and *Live Sentence* (1984). He then formed his own band, Rising Force, which toured extensively and released *Marching Out* (1985), *Trilogy* (1986) and *Odyssey* (1988), each of which expanded his following. Malmsteen recruited Swedish musicians for his next band. *Eclipse* (1990), *Fire & Ice* (1992), *The Seventh Sign* (1994) and *Magnum Opus* (1995) were major successes in Japan. *Inspiration* (1996) paid tribute to Malmsteen's influences, covering songs by Deep Purple, Hendrix, Rush and The Scorpions. In 1998 he recorded the 'Concerto Suite For Electric Guitar And Orchestra' with the Czech Philharmonic Orchestra. He also revived Rising Force for *Unleash The Fury* (2005) and released the acoustic instrumental album *Angels Of Love* in 2009.

**DATE OF BIRTH**

30 June 1963

**PLACE OF BIRTH**

Stockholm, Sweden

**GENRES**

Neo-Classical Rock, Power Metal

# JOHNNY MARR

## BONA FIDE BRITISH LEGEND

Indie guitar legend Johnny Marr grew up in a household where music was a constant fixture, and his influences ranged from Howlin' Wolf to Jimmy Page, Bert Jansch and Rory Gallagher. In 1982 Marr teamed up with Steven Morrissey, giving birth to The Smiths, and in short order they became the most influential indie group of the Eighties. Marr aimed to serve the song rather than his ego and took only two solos in the entire Smiths' canon, on the single 'Shoplifters Of The World Unite' and on 'Paint A Vulgar Picture' from *Strangeways, Here We Come* (1987).

Marr left The Smiths in 1987, frustrated with the direction of the group. He went on to work with artists including Bryan Ferry, Billy Bragg, Pet Shop Boys, Talking Heads and one of his heroes, Bert Jansch, on his album *Crimson Moon* (2000). In 1991 he formed Electronic with Bernard Sumner, an occasional pairing that produced three albums. In 2001, Marr put together his own band The Healers, handling lead vocals for the first time on *Boomslang* (2003). He became a member of US indie band Modest Mouse in 2006, appearing on the album *We Were Dead Before The Ship Even Sank* (2007), an American No. 1. In 2008 he teamed up with The Cribs and became a full-time member for their 2009 album, *Ignore the Ignorant*.

### DATE OF BIRTH

31 October 1963

### PLACE OF BIRTH

Manchester, England

### GENRES

Indie, Alternative Rock

# JUAN MARTÍN

## USING THE GUITAR TO PAINT

Juan Cristóbal Martín started learning the guitar at the age of six. In his early twenties he moved to Madrid to study under Nino Ricardo and Paco de Lucía. His major influences included de Lucía, Tomatito and Andrés Segovia, but his work also evokes jazz guitarists such as Joe Pass and even the late Brazilian guitar virtuoso Laurindo Almeida. One of Martín's early recordings was *Picasso Portraits* (1981), each section of which is an audio depiction of a painting by Pablo Picasso.

Martín began his recording career in the Eighties, when he recorded albums for RCA's Novus label, including *Through The Moving Window* and *Painter In Sound* (both released 1990). Martín crossed paths with jazz greats ranging from tenor and soprano saxophonist Wayne Shorter to Brazilian singer Flora Purim and her percussionist husband, Airto Moreira. Martín recorded for the Alex label in the early to mid–Nineties, and in the late Nineties and early Noughties recorded extensively for the independent Flamenco Vision imprint. By early 2005 Martín had recorded at least 16 albums. He has been voted in the top three guitarists in the world in the magazine *Guitar Player*. His latest albums have flamenco dancers on the soundtrack, adding the sounds of flamenco *zapateado* dancing to the music.

**DATE OF BIRTH**

1948

**PLACE OF BIRTH**

Málaga, Spain

**GENRES**

Flamenco

# JOHN MARTYN

## GRACE AND GLORY

John Martyn blended blues and folk into a unique style, working in the London folk scene of the mid-Sixties. He signed to Island Records and released his first album, *London Conversation*, in 1968. By 1970 Martyn had incorporated jazz into his work and developed a unique acoustic guitar sound using effects boxes. This was first apparent on *Stormbringer* in 1970, which featured Martyn's then wife, Beverley Kutner. In 1973 Martyn released *Solid Air*, which included 'May You Never', perhaps his best-known song. Following this success, Martyn became experimental with *Inside Out* (1974), pensive with *Sunday's Child* (1975) and a naturalist with *One World* (1977).

Martyn's break-up with Beverley resulted in the heart-wrenching *Grace And Danger* (1980). A deluxe double-disc re-master of the album was released in 2007. Phil Collins played drums and sang backing vocals on *Grace And Danger* and produced Martyn's next album, *Glorious Fool* (1981). Martyn left Island in 1981 and has recorded sporadically since then. In July 2006 the documentary *Johnny Too Bad* documented the period surrounding the operation to amputate John's right leg below the knee and the recording of *On The Cobbles* (2004). In 2008 Martyn received the lifetime achievement award at the BBC Radio 2 Folk Awards. He sadly passed away on 29 January 2009 as a result of double pneumonia.

### DATE OF BIRTH/DEATH

11 September 1948/29 January 2009

### PLACE OF BIRTH

New Malden, England

### GENRES

Folk

A-Z OF GUITAR GODS

# HANK MARVIN

## OUT OF THE SHADOWS

Britain's first home-grown guitar hero Hank Marvin formed a skiffle band, The Railroaders, with school friend Bruce Welch. They travelled to London in 1958 and gravitated to the legendary 2i's coffee bar, where they were recruited to play in Cliff Richard's backing band The Drifters. The band also recorded in its own right and, after a change of name to The Shadows, their fourth single, 'Apache' (1960), reached No. 1 – a huge influnce on hip-hop in the Seventies and the first of a string of instrumental hits characterized by Marvin's echoing lead lines and manipulation of the tremolo arm. Richard and The Shadows' combined output dominated the British pop charts in the period immediately prior to The Beatles, and while the Shadows survived the arrival of Merseybeat, their popularity began to wane in the mid–Sixties.

After The Shadows split up in 1968, Marvin made a self–titled solo album and then formed the vocal–harmony trio Marvin, Welch & Farrar, which developed into a revived version of The Shadows. The new line-up's debut, *Rocking With Curly Leads* (1973), saw Marvin experimenting with a vocoder. By the Eighties, The Shadows' output consisted mainly of cover versions. In 1990, Marvin resumed his occasional solo career, and The Shadows reunited for a farewell tour in 2004–05, only to reconvene in 2009 for another tour and new album, *Reunited: Cliff Richard And The Shadows*.

**DATE OF BIRTH**

28 October 1941

**PLACE OF BIRTH**

Newcastle-upon-Tyne, England

**GENRES**

Rock, Pop

A-Z OF GUITAR GODS

# BRIAN MAY

## QUEEN'S GUITAR KING

Brian May achieved immortality alongside Roger Taylor, Freddie Mercury and John Deacon in the ultimate glam rock band Queen. They took the music scene by storm with their self-titled debut in 1973, and brought their stylish hard rock into focus with *Sheer Heart Attack* (1974). With *A Night At The Opera* (1975) Queen moved into a theatrical pop style and the operatic 'Bohemian Rhapsody' – with May's memorable solo – became a global hit. A succession of killer discs followed, including *A Day At The Races* (1976), *Jazz* (1978) and *Hot Space* (1982), for which May wrote three tracks, including the single 'Las Palabras de Amor'. After an extended break in 1983, Queen reconvened to record *The Works* (1984) and then *A Kind Of Magic* (1986), with May writing and arranging the orchestra parts for 'Who Wants To Live Forever'.

After Mercury's death May completed the solo *Back To The Light* in 1992 and then worked with Deacon and Taylor, completing songs for which Mercury had already recorded vocals, on *Made In Heaven* (1995). A second solo album followed, *Another World* (1998). In 2004 May and Taylor began working with Paul Rodgers as Queen + Paul Rodgers, and they released their only album, *The Cosmos Rocks*, in 2008 before splitting up the following year.

**DATE OF BIRTH**

19 July 1947

**PLACE OF BIRTH**

Hampton, England

**GENRES**

Hard Rock, Progressive Rock, Glam Rock

A-Z OF
GUITAR GODS

# MIKE McCREADY

## PEARL JAMMER

Mike McCready was 11 when he bought his first guitar and began to take lessons. In high school he formed a band that disintegrated after failing to secure a record contract in Los Angeles. McCready was working with rhythm guitarist Stone Gossard when the pair were invited to participate in recording *Temple Of The Dog* (1991), a one-off project founded by Soundgarden singer Chris Cornell. McCready's solo on 'Reach Down' remains one of his proudest achievements. Shortly after recording *Temple Of The Dog*, McCready and Gossard formed Pearl Jam with Eddie Vedder and Jeff Ament. Their debut, *Ten* (1991), was lyrically dark, combining classic rock with an anthemic feel, informed by McCready's love of the blues in his prominent solos.

Pearl Jam were associated with the Seattle grunge scene, but were accused by their contemporaries of cashing in on the alternative rock boom. The band seemed uneasy with their own success and rebelled against music industry practices, refusing to appear in music videos and boycotting the booking agency Ticketmaster. McCready fought his own battles against drug and alcohol addiction. He has participated in various side projects, including Mad Season, The Rockfords and UFO–tribute act Flight To Mars, while Pearl Jam's music is currently being reissued and the band released a new album, *Backpacker*, in 2009.

**DATE OF BIRTH**

5 April 1966

**PLACE OF BIRTH**

Pensacola, USA

**GENRES**

Grunge, Alternative Rock, Hard Rock

A–Z OF
GUITAR GODS

# ROGER McGUINN

## SIGNATURE SOUNDS

James Joseph McGuinn was raised in Chicago and became a fan of folk music as a teenager. At Chicago's Old Town School of Folk Music his skills attracted the attention of recording artists and, by 1964, he had been a member of The Limeliters, The Chad Mitchell Trio and Bobby Darin's band. He recorded with Hoyt Axton, Judy Collins and a young duo named Tom & Jerry, soon to become Simon & Garfunkel.

After relocating to LA, McGuinn met singer–guitarist David Crosby and singer–songwriter Gene Clark. Adding bassist Chris Hillman and drummer Michael Clarke, they formed The Byrds, wanting to bring elements of the British Invasion sound to the folk–influenced songs of Bob Dylan and the band's writers. The first single, 'Mr Tambourine Man', featured McGuinn's new, revolutionary guitar sound: a Rickenbacker 12–string heavily compressed to create a jingly sustain that influenced guitarists for decades. Along the way Jim McGuinn was renamed Roger by the founder of the Subud spiritual group. After The Byrds split McGuinn continued to tour and release solo albums. In 2005 he released a box set containing 100 of his favourite songs from the Folk Den, following it up with another 22 selections on a 2008 collection.

**DATE OF BIRTH**

13 July 1942

**PLACE OF BIRTH**

Chicago, USA

**GENRES**

Folk Rock, Country Rock

# JOHN McLAUGHLIN

## INSPIRATION AND DEVOTION

John McLaughlin worked with Alexis Korner, Graham Bond, Ginger Baker and others in the Sixties and released his first album, *Extrapolation*, in 1969. He turned to Indian influences for *My Goals Beyond* (1970) and took the name Mahavishnu. In 1969 McLaughlin moved to New York and was a member of Miles Davis's band for several successful releases, including *In A Silent Way* (1969) and *A Tribute To Jack Johnson* (1970). In 1971 he formed The Mahavishnu Orchestra, a group with a rock image but with the sophisticated vocabulary of jazz.

In the mid-Seventies McLaughlin surprised the music world by radically shifting direction, switching to acoustic guitar and playing Indian music with his group Shakti. In 1979 McLaughlin formed the short-lived Trio Of Doom and later led the One Truth Band. He played in trios with Al Di Meola and Paco de Lucía, reformed The Mahavishnu Orchestra and toured with a jazz trio featuring organist Joey DeFrancesco and drummer Dennis Chambers. In recent years McLaughlin has created a ballet score, *Thieves And Poets*, and scored arrangements of jazz standards for classical guitar ensembles. In 2007, he joined the internet-based Abstract Logix label, which works with independent jazz, progressive rock and world-music bands. He also toured with a new jazz-fusion quartet, The 4th Dimension, and formed Five Peace Band with jazz legends Chick Corea and Kenny Garrett, for a 2009 tour.

**DATE OF BIRTH**

4 January 1942

**PLACE OF BIRTH**

Doncaster, England

**GENRES**

Jazz Fusion, World, Classical

# PAT METHENY

## PIONEER AND VISIONARY

Born in Kansas City, Missouri, Metheny began playing trumpet by the age of eight and switched to guitar at 12. By the age of 15, he was gigging regularly with the hottest jazz players in the area. He hit the international scene in 1974, playing with the great vibraphonist Gary Burton. Already, his loose and flexible articulation, reminiscent of sax greats such as Charlie Parker and John Coltrane, was on full display. In 1976 Metheny released his solo debut, *Bright Size Life*, which introduced the 'chorused' sound, achieved via delay effects and multiple amplifiers. It would become the traditional jazz-guitar sound for a whole new generation of players. In 1979 he became the first jazz guitarist to use the guitar-synthesizer (Roland GR-300) in an improvisational setting. He was also instrumental in the development of the soprano acoustic guitar, his own signature Ibanez PM-100 guitar and various other custom instruments.

More than just a jazz-guitar virtuoso, Metheny has performed with an impressively diverse range of artists, including Steve Reich, Ornette Coleman, Joni Mitchell, Herbie Hancock and David Bowie. And as a composer, his curriculum vitae includes compositions for solo guitar, small ensembles and large orchestras in settings ranging from modern jazz to rock to classical to ballet. His latest album, *Orchestration* (2010), saw Metheny use the eponymous machine to record a whole orchestra of instruments in real time, all under his own control.

**DATE OF BIRTH**

12 August 1954

**PLACE OF BIRTH**

Kasas City, USA

**GENRES**

Jazz Fusion, Contemporary Jazz

A-Z OF
GUITAR GODS

# WES MONTGOMERY

## THE BOSS GUITAR

Wes Montgomery emerged in the Fifties and gained a wide following in the cool jazz movement before turning to pop jazz in the Sixties. With his unique use of lead lines played in octaves with his left hand and strummed by his right-hand thumb, Montgomery mixed jazz harmonies with R&B rhythms to gain a pop following and exert broad influence on later pop-jazz guitarists such as George Benson.

Montgomery toured and recorded with Lionel Hampton from 1948 to 1950. Cannonball Adderley helped him to find a recording contract and recorded with him on *Poll Winners* (1960). John Coltrane asked Montgomery to join his band, but Montgomery continued to lead his own outfit, thus earning his nickname Boss Guitar. *The Incredible Jazz Guitar Of Wes Montgomery* (1960) featured one of his best-known compositions, 'Four On Six'. In 1964 he moved to Verve Records, and his music started to shift towards pop. He didn't abandon jazz entirely, however, and both *The Dynamic Duo* (1966) and *The Further Adventures Of Jimmy And Wes* (1966) show his ability to blend R&B and pop elements with jazz. In the late Sixties, Montgomery turned to jazzy versions of pop-rock tunes with orchestral arrangements and enjoyed the greatest success of his career, before dying of a heart attack in 1968.

### DATE OF BIRTH/DEATH

6 March 1925/15 June 1968

### PLACE OF BIRTH

Indianapolis, USA

### GENRES

Pop Jazz, Cool Jazz, Contemporary Jazz

# CARLOS MONTOYA

## FLAMENCO FINGER-PICKING HERO

Born into a gypsy family in Spain, Montoya began playing live in the Twenties and Thirties. At the beginning of the Second World War he was on tour in the United States and decided to settle in New York. In 1948 Montoya began playing with symphonies and orchestras and performing guitar recitals. He became the first flamenco guitarist to tour the world as a guest performer with orchestras. His appearances expanded to television and recording, with more than 40 albums, some with orchestras, completed. His reissued albums on CD include *The Art Of Flamenco* (1993), *Flamenco* (1996) and *Flamenco Direct* (1990).

Montoya had many critics and detractors among purists and serious scholars of Spanish guitar. Because flamenco is grounded traditionally as an accompaniment for dancers, maintaining a solid rhythm, or *compas*, on guitar is fundamental. Montoya's excursions into varying dynamics and time changes on classics such as 'Malagueña', which Montoya filled with rapid-fire hammer-ons and pull-offs, sometimes at the expense of precise fingering, got him categorized as a flashy showman. But fans around the world fell in love with the emotion and fiery romance suggested by his playing. Montoya died of heart failure at the age of 89 in Wainscott, NY.

### DATE OF BIRTH/DEATH

13 December 1903/3 March 1993

### PLACE OF BIRTH

Madrid, Spain

### GENRES

Flamenco

# GARY MOORE

## SKID ROW TO SOLO

In 1969 Gary Moore joined Skid Row, an Irish blues–rock group that featured Phil Lynott on vocals. When the latter was sacked, Moore took over as singer. Skid Row supported Fleetwood Mac, then featuring Peter Green. With Green's help, the band signed a contract with CBS, releasing two influential albums before Moore left in 1971. His debut album *Grinding Stone* (1973) was credited to The Gary Moore Band, but his initial solo career was short–lived, as he was reunited with Phil Lynott, replacing Eric Bell as Thin Lizzy's lead guitarist.

With a little help from Lynott on vocals, Moore's solo career resumed in 1979, when his distinctive bluesy, wailing guitar graced the singles chart on 'Parisienne Walkways'. The pair charted again with the heavier 'Out In The Fields' in 1985. The Eighties saw Moore concentrating on rock, but he returned to his first love on *Still Got The Blues* (1990). After some puzzling experiments with dance beats, he went back to basics once more on *Back To The Blues* (2001), and has released several albums since, the most recent being *Bad For You Baby* (2008). Of the many guitars that he has used in his lengthy career, Moore is probably most attached to the Gibson Les Paul that he bought from his mentor Peter Green when the latter quit the music business.

**DATE OF BIRTH**

4 April 1952

**PLACE OF BIRTH**

Belfast, Northern Ireland

**GENRES**

Blues, Hard Rock

# SCOTTY MOORE

## LEADING THE FIELD

In 1952 Scotty Moore (pictured left) and Bill Black formed The Starlite Wranglers and persuaded Sam Phillips, the proprietor of Memphis label Sun Records, to let them record. Phillips subsequently suggested that Moore and Black accompany his protégé, Elvis Presley (pictured right). Arthur Crudup's 'That's All Right, Mama' captured the chemistry between them and in 1954 became Presley's first single. Moore and Black, along with drummer D.J. Fontana, backed Elvis on his greatest records. Before Chuck Berry and Bo Diddley, Moore fused various strands of American music to create the language of rock'n'roll lead guitar, establishing it as the main instrument and inspiring countless guitarists since. Moore favoured Gibson guitars, using the semi-acoustic ES-295 on early Sun recordings with Presley and switching in 1955 to an L5 and later to a Super 400 CES for 'Jailhouse Rock' and 'King Creole'.

Moore backed Elvis until 1958, although he and Black had temporarily quit a year earlier in a dispute over money. He made his only solo album, the all-instrumental *The Guitar That Changed The World* (1964), and worked with Presley again during the Sixties. Afterwards, Scotty virtually retired from playing for 23 years, founding his own recording studio in Memphis and concentrating on engineering records and television productions.

**DATE OF BIRTH**

27 December, 1931

**PLACE OF BIRTH**

Gadsen, USA

**GENRES**

Rock'n'Roll

# THURSTON MOORE
## SONIC YOUTH'S GROUNDBREAKER

While playing in a band called the Coachmen in New York, Thurston met Lee Ranaldo, an art student and member of Glenn Branca's avant-garde guitar orchestra. The pair, along with Moore's future wife Kim Gordon, formed the core of Sonic Youth, which became part of New York's No Wave experimental scene. The band's early work was released on a variety of independent labels. *Bad Moon Rising* (1985) was their first album to be distributed widely in America, where it was largely ignored, and in the UK, where it received critical acclaim and encouraging sales. Switching to the influential independent label STT, Sonic Youth produced what is arguably their masterpiece, *Daydream Nation* (1988), before moving to Geffen.

Sonic Youth are one of the most original guitar bands of all time due to the twin guitars of Moore and Ranaldo, which characterized their sound. They were influenced by Glenn Branca, Can, Velvet Underground, The Patti Smith Group and The Stooges, as well as the speed and intensity of early Eighties hardcore punk bands Bad Brains, Minor Threat and Black Flag. In turn, Sonic Youth were hailed as the godfathers of the American alternative scene, which went mainstream in the early Nineties, and were a major influence on Kurt Cobain and Nirvana. They released their most recent album, *The Eternal*, in 2009, while Moore continues to record with various side projects such as noise jazzers Original Silence.

**DATE OF BIRTH**

25 July 1958

**PLACE OF BIRTH**

Coral Gables, USA

**GENRES**

Alternative Rock, No Wave

A-Z OF
GUITAR GODS

# STEVE MORSE

## DIXIE DREGS TO DEEP PURPLE

A consummate guitarist in an extraordinary variety of styles, Steve Morse learned piano, clarinet and violin before picking up the guitar. He and bassist Andy West formed Dixie Grit, a heavy metal covers band, in the late Sixties. They later took part in a musical lab project called Rock Ensemble II, which became The Dixie Dregs, playing a mixture of jazz rock and Southern rock. *Free Fall* (1977), *What If* (1978) and *Dregs Of The Earth* (1980) were critically praised, but even Grammy nominations couldn't generate commercial sales, and the group disbanded in 1983. Morse formed his own trio out of The Dixie Dregs and released *The Introduction* (1984) and *Stand Up* (1985). Resuming his solo career, Morse expanded his own parameters on albums such as *High Tension Wires* (1989), *Southern Steel* (1991) and *Coast To Coast* (1992), while participating in The Dixie Dregs revival on *Bring 'Em Back Alive* (1992) and *Full Circle* (1994).

In 1994 Morse replaced Ritchie Blackmore in Deep Purple and has remained their guitarist, consolidating his role on *Abandon* (1998), *Total Abandon* (1999), *Bananas* (2003) and *Raptures Of The Deep* (2005). Morse has also maintained his solo career with *Major Impacts* (2000), *Split Decision* (2002) and *Major Impacts II* (2004). His Angelfire collaboration with Sarah Spencer is due for release in 2010.

**DATE OF BIRTH**

28 July 1954

**PLACE OF BIRTH**

Hamilton, USA

**GENRES**

Rock, Country, Classical, Funk, Jazz, Fusion

# BOB MOULD

## GODFATHER OF GRUNGE

Bob Mould was 16 when, inspired by the Ramones, he took up guitar. While attending college in Minnesota in 1979 he founded Hüsker Dü, which was instrumental in establishing alternative rock in America. Signing to Warner Brothers in 1986, they made *Candy Apple Grey* (1986) and *Warehouse: Songs And Stories* (1987), which, although popular on college radio, failed to bring them to a wider audience. The band split in 1988 because of drug problems and the ongoing tensions between Mould and Grant Hart, the group's other songwriter and vocalist.

Mould launched a solo career with *Workbook* (1989). His characteristic wall-of-guitars sound was largely replaced by a more reflective, acoustic ambience. *Black Sheets Of Rain* (1991) returned him to familiar guitar-heavy terrain, which continued in Mould's new band Sugar, whose debut *Copper Blue* (1992) received widespread acclaim. The mini-album *Beaster* (1993) was notable for the angst-ridden 'JC Auto' on which Mould's powerful playing achieved climactic momentum. After *File Under: Easy Listening* (1994), he disbanded Sugar and resumed his solo career. *DJ. Modulate* (2002) and *Body Of Song* (2005) added electronica to his rock template, while *Long Playing Grooves* (2002) was a full-on dance album released under the pseudonym LoudBomb. *Life And Times* (2009) was a return to guitar-based albums.

**DATE OF BIRTH**

16 October 1960

**PLACE OF BIRTH**

Malone, USA

**GENRES**

Alternative Rock, Punk, Dance

# MUDDY WATERS

## BRIDGING DELTA AND CHICAGO

Muddy Waters is the vital link between the pre-war Delta blues and the post-war Chicago blues. Born in Mississippi, he moved to Chicago in 1943 and by 1948, when he had his first local hit with 'I Can't Be Satisfied', his guitar playing had developed a trademark style, bringing a more aggressive quality to his single-note Delta riffs and slide technique. Waters built a powerful reputation in Chicago's clubs and bars, and recorded a series of songs that would become Chicago blues anthems: 'I Just Want To Make Love To You', 'I'm Ready' and 'I'm Your Hoochie Coochie Man'. The last two used a variation on the call-and-response songs from the Delta plantations, with Waters filling in the spaces with moaning vocals or stinging guitar breaks.

Waters took advantage of the British blues boom of the Sixties to broaden his audience, touring the UK and Europe and recording *The London Muddy Waters Sessions* (1971) with Rory Gallagher and Georgie Fame. During the Seventies he toured with The Rolling Stones and Eric Clapton, and appeared in The Band's 'The Last Waltz' concert and film. His record career was revived in the late Seventies with a trio of Johnny Winter-produced albums: *Hard Again* (1977), *I'm Ready* (1978) and *King Bee* (1981).

### DATE OF BIRTH/DEATH

4 April 1913/30 April 1983

### PLACE OF BIRTH

Rolling Fork, USA

### GENRES

Chicago Blues, Electric Blues

# DAVE MURRAY

## IRON MAIDEN TO ICON 2

Inspired by the early rock sounds of Jimi Hendrix, Free and Deep Purple, Dave Murray got his first guitar at the age of 15 and started a band called Stone Free, which also contained future Maiden guitarist Adrian Smith. In 1976, he met Steve Harris, who asked him to join his fledgling metal band, Iron Maiden, and after some delay Murray accepted the gig. In 1980, they released their eponymous debut, followed in 1981 by *Killers*. Metal guitarists still cite these as among the most influential albums of all time. But in terms of worldwide superstardom, it was the arrival of singer Bruce Dickinson and Maiden's subsequent string of amazing albums, including *Number Of The Beast* (1982), *Piece Of Mind* (1983) and *Powerslave* (1984), which put the band on top of the world.

During this time of exploding publicity and recognition, Murray began to garner increasing coverage in guitar magazines and metal–based fanzines, his 1957 black Fender Strat ubiquitously present. Though subsequent album sales gradually faded, Iron Maiden's appeal as a live act has never waned. From their 1984 World Slavery Tour, which saw them play 322 gigs in 20 countries, to headlining countless festivals, Iron Maiden has by unofficial count entertained more fans than any band in music history. A summer American tour is set for 2010 to coincide with new album, *The Final Frontier*.

**DATE OF BIRTH**

23 December 1956

**PLACE OF BIRTH**

London, England

**GENRES**

Heavy Metal

A–Z OF
GUITAR GODS

# DAVE NAVARRO

## MASTER OF ADDICTION

Dave Navarro began playing guitar at the age of seven and was in various bands in school. In 1986, he joined Jane's Addiction on the recommendation of drummer Stephen Perkins, a childhood friend. The band quickly gained a following in Los Angeles and released their first album, *Jane's Addiction* (1987), independently. A live set with copious studio overdubs, the album was an unpredictable mix of folk, rock, funk and new wave punctuated by Navarro's unusual, angular guitar (a PRS). Their second album for Warner Brothers, *Ritual De Lo Habitual* (1990), provided their breakthrough and is regarded as the band's masterpiece. Navarro's solo on 'Three Days' is one of his finest. After the trail-blazing Lollapalooza tour in 1991, Jane's Addiction split up.

Navarro formed Deconstruction, whose sole album *Deconstruction* (1994) is now a cult classic, before joining Red Hot Chili Peppers. After one album, *One Hot Minute* (1995), Navarro was dismissed due to creative differences. He participated in a Jane's Addiction tour in 1997, and the band reunited again in 2001. In between he worked with artists as diverse as Marilyn Manson and Christina Aguilera. He has co-hosted MTV's reality show *Rock Star*, has since put together a new band, the Panic Channel, and tours a mix of guitar and hip-hop around America with DJ Skribble.

**DATE OF BIRTH**

7 June 1967

**PLACE OF BIRTH**

Santa Monica, USA

**GENRES**

Alternative Rock, Hard Rock

# RICK NIELSEN

## NO CHEAP TRICKS HERE

As lead guitarist and primary songwriter of the rock band Cheap Trick, Rick Nielsen fired the band's melting pot of pop melodies and punk energy. The band was signed by Epic in 1976, and released its self-titled album in February 1977. Neither the debut nor their next two albums, *In Color* (1977) and *Heaven Tonight* (1978), were well received, although *Heaven Tonight*, with its teen anthem 'Surrender', is now considered by many to be the group's best album. Cheap Trick's real strength was their live show and, on tour in Japan in 1978, they recorded the breakthrough live album *At Budokan*. By the spring of 1979 it was No. 4 on the US Top 40 album charts, fuelled by the single 'I Want You To Want Me', written by Nielsen. He performed on Alice Cooper's *From The Inside* (1978), Hall & Oates' *Along The Red Ledge* (1978) and the sessions for John Lennon's album *Double Fantasy* (1980).

Nielsen's unique guitars, including a five-necked monster, have been stars of the band's shows. Nielsen has collaborated with guitar manufacturer Hamer on several 'themed' guitars, including the Rockford and Doctor models.

**DATE OF BIRTH**

22 December 1946

**PLACE OF BIRTH**

Rockford, USA

**GENRES**

Rock, Pop, Hard Rock

# TED NUGENT
## MOTOR CITY MADMAN

Ted Nugent gained fame as the lead guitarist of The Amboy Dukes, although as a lifelong conservative with a distaste for drugs and drinking, he didn't fit the image championed by the Dukes' psychedelic material. The band issued three albums before Nugent departed. By the mid–Seventies Nugent was a solo artist with a stage show that wowed the metal crowd. With the release of *Cat Scratch Fever* (1975) he rose to the top of the charts and 1978's *Double Live Gonzo!* cemented his success. But over the course of his next three albums – *Weekend Warriors* (1978), *State of Shock* (1979) and *Scream Dream* (1980) – Nugent was driven into bankruptcy.

Nugent released a series of albums that failed to catch fire in the Eighties. He tried his hand at acting and became known as much for his right–wing views as for his music. By the end of the decade he had joined the rock supergroup Damn Yankees, which scored a surprise hit with 'High Enough' from their self–titled 1990 album. The band dissolved, however, after one more release. Nugent became a solo act again, turning out the well–received *Spirit Of The Wild* (1995). He has continued to tour, and his third live collection, *Full Bluntal Nugity*, was released in 2001. He has since become something of a reality TV star, though his latest venture, *Runnin' Wild... From Ted Nugent*, in which Nugent and his son hunt down contestants in a survival game show, is yet to run.

### DATE OF BIRTH

13 December 1948

### PLACE OF BIRTH

Detroit, USA

### GENRES

Rock, Hard Rock, Heavy Metal

# MIKE OLDFIELD

## INNOVATIVE INSTRUMENTALIST

For 35 years Mike Oldfield melded all manner of musical genres, from classical to progressive rock. In 1967 he and his sister Sally formed the folk duo Sallyangie and were signed to Transatlantic Records. In 1970 he joined ex-Soft Machine vocalist Kevin Ayers' backing group The Whole World. He had composed the music for *Tubular Bells*, but Oldfield's early version was called unmarketable by several labels. However, in 1972 Richard Branson signed him to his new Virgin Records, and Oldfield began recording. The disc broke new ground as an instrumental concept album and earned Oldfield a Grammy.

The early Eighties saw Oldfield make a transition to 'mainstream' popular music, with a string of collaborations featuring various lead vocalists alongside his characteristic, searing guitar solos. The best known of these songs is 'Moonlight Shadow', his 1983 hit with Maggie Reilly. Oldfield later turned to film and video, writing the score for Roland Joffé's acclaimed film *The Killing Fields*. He has explored a variety of themes and musical ideas, from Celtic-themed albums to instrumental and pop song pairings and from new-age explorations to re-imaginings of *Tubular Bells*. In 1999 he released *Guitars*, which used guitars as the source for all the sounds on the album, including percussion, while *Music Of The Spheres* (2008) was his first classical album.

**DATE OF BIRTH**

15 May 1953

**PLACE OF BIRTH**

Reading, England

**GENRES**

Ambient, Classical, World, Electronic, Pop, Progressive Rock

# JIMMY PAGE
## YARDBIRDS TO LED ZEPPELIN

Jimmy Page became an icon of rock guitar with Led Zeppelin. Early in his career he was an in-demand session musician before joining The Yardbirds in 1966. However, he soon found himself carrying an increasingly disillusioned band. Page, Robert Plant, John Paul Jones and John Bonham came together in 1968 and recorded *Led Zeppelin* (1969), which made a resounding impact. *Led Zeppelin II* (1969) followed, but with *Led Zeppelin III* (1970) the band put more emphasis on the arrangements. This approach paid off spectacularly on *Led Zeppelin IV*, otherwise entitled or known as *Four Symbols* (1971). Through the mid-Seventies they swept all before them with *Houses Of The Holy* (1973), *Physical Graffiti* (1975), *Presence* (1976) and *The Song Remains The Same* (1976), but in 1977 the band's career came to a halt when Plant's son died suddenly. They returned in 1979, but the following year Bonham died after a drinking binge and Led Zeppelin was at an end.

During the Eighties and Nineties Page occupied himself with the film soundtracks, solo albums and notable collaborations with Robert Plant and The Black Crowes, but in 2007 Led Zeppelin reformed with Bonham's son Jason on drums to play a spectacular show at London's $O_2$ Arena. Page is rumoured to be underatking a solo tour in 2010.

### DATE OF BIRTH

9 January 1944

### PLACE OF BIRTH

Heston, England

### GENRES

Hard Rock, Heavy Metal, Blues Rock, Folk Rock

# JOE PASS
## JAZZ VIRTUOSO

California native Joe Pass developed a thoroughly precise jazz technique that propelled him to virtuoso status alongside pianist Oscar Peterson and vocalist Ella Fitzgerald, with whom he made a series of essential recordings for the Pablo label in the Seventies. Pass began his career travelling with small jazz groups and recorded a series of albums for the Pacific Jazz label, receiving *Downbeat* magazine's New Star Award in 1963. He played on recordings by various artists, but his main gig in the Sixties was TV and recording–session work in Los Angeles. He was a sideman with Frank Sinatra, Sarah Vaughan and others, and worked in many of the bands of late–night TV talk shows. Producer Norman Granz signed Pass to Pablo Records in 1970. In 1974 Pass released his landmark solo album *Virtuoso*. The same year, Pablo released the album *The Trio*, which featured Pass, Oscar Peterson and Niels–Henning Ørsted Pedersen and won a Grammy for Best Jazz Performance.

Pass used an amazing jazz vocabulary and a command of dynamics and tempo, combined with a sophisticated harmonic sense and a knack for creating counterpoint between improvised lead lines. Pass played a Gibson ES–175 guitar and later a guitar made for him by master crafter Jimmy D'Aquisto.

### DATE OF BIRTH/DEATH

13 January 1929/23 May 1994

### PLACE OF BIRTH

New Brunswick, USA

### GENRES

Jazz

# CHARLEY PATTON

## DELTA BLUES PIONEER

The first great Delta–blues singer, Charley Patton grew up listening to field hollers and levee–camp moans as well as gospel, ragtime, country, folk and novelty songs. By the early Twenties he had several distinctive songs in his repertoire, including 'Pea Vine Blues', 'Spoonful Blues', 'Mississippi Boweavil Blues' and his signature tune, the socially aspiring 'Pony Blues'. He was an extrovert showman, playing his guitar behind his back or with his teeth and hitting the guitar body for rhythmic emphasis. He was already a local legend by the time he made his first recordings (including 'Pony Blues') in 1929. It was backed by 'Banty Rooster Blues', a description that could have applied to Patton himself, a snappy dresser who had several wives.

By his final recording session early in 1934, Patton's lifestyle was beginning to catch up with him. His voice had deteriorated after his throat was slashed (reportedly in a fight over a woman) the previous year, and the songs included two religious numbers performed with his then wife, Bertha Lee. Patton died later that year from a heart attack, but his raw, driving and percussive kind of guitar playing was a seminal influence on the following generation of Mississippi blues singers.

**DATE OF BIRTH/DEATH**

1 May 1891/28 April 1934

**PLACE OF BIRTH**

Edwards, USA

**GENRES**

Delta Blues

# LES PAUL

## INNOVATOR AND ICON

Performer and innovator Les Paul (pictured left, beside B.B. King) was playing guitar and experimenting with sound by the time he was 11. By 18 he was playing country music under the name Rhubarb Red. After hearing Django Reinhardt, he switched over to jazz and changed his name to Les Paul. In 1943, after a successful stint on New York radio, Paul moved to Hollywood, formed a trio, and began appearing with stars such as Nat 'King' Cole and Bing Crosby, with whom he recorded a hit version of 'It's Been A Long, Long Time'. Crosby helped finance Paul's experiments, which resulted in the Gibson Guitar Company adopting Paul's suggestions for a guitar that later became the Les Paul model.

In 1947, Capitol Records released a recording that had begun as an experiment in Paul's garage. It featured Paul playing eight different parts on electric guitar. Paul's experiments initiated the process of multitrack recording, which he used to successful effect when he teamed with singer Mary Ford for a string of Fifties hits such as 'How High The Moon'. Paul's fame helped his namesake guitar gain fans, exploding in popularity in the rock era. Paul continued to innovate and perform, and in the twenty-first century the 90-year-old legend still held down a weekly gig in New York. He finally passed away after suffering from complications with pneumonia, on 12 August 2009.

### DATE OF BIRTH/DEATH

9 June 1915/12 August 2009

### PLACE OF BIRTH

Waukesha, USA

### GENRES

Jazz, Blues

# JOE PERRY
## A TOXIC TWIN

Joe Perry (pictured left) projects a swagger and ultra-cool stage presence that few guitarists can match. Fewer still possess his capacity for muscular, gritty soloing and hook-laden riffing, played on his signature Gibson Les Paul. In 1969, while playing in The Jam Band, Perry met singer Steven Tyler (pictured right), and thus Aerosmith and the 'Toxic Twins' were born. Their albums *Toys In The Attic* (1975) and *Rocks* (1976) are generally recognized as two of the most important hard-rock albums of the Seventies, producing such timeless hits as 'Walk This Way', 'Sweet Emotion' and 'Back In The Saddle'. But heavy drug and alcohol abuse led to Aerosmith's demise in 1979.

In 1980, working as The Joe Perry Project, the guitarist released *Let The Music Do The Talking*, an underrated album of incendiary guitar work. After two more Project albums, Perry rejoined the original Aerosmith line-up for a reunion tour. A collaboration with rap group Run-DMC on the classic hit 'Walk This Way' put the Toxic Twins back on the mainstream map. They would subsequently sober up and go on to huge success with *Permanent Vacation* (1987), *Pump* (1989) and *Get a Grip* (1993). Perry himself continued to work on solo projects, including 2005's *Joe Perry* and 2009's Joe Perry Project album, *Have Guitar, Will Travel*.

### DATE OF BIRTH

10 September 1950

### PLACE OF BIRTH

Lawrence, USA

### GENRES

Hard Rock, Heavy Metal, Blues Rock

# JOHN PETRUCCI
## DREAM THEATER TO G3

The guitarist in Dream Theater, John Petrucci started played guitar at the age of 12 and assiduously practised and emulated his heroes, from Steve Howe to Randy Rhoads. At 18 he attended Berklee College of Music in Boston with his school friend, bassist John Myung. There they met drummer Mike Portnoy and formed the basis of Dream Theater. Recruiting keyboard player Kevin Moore and singer Charlie Dominici, they released *When Dream And Day Unite* (1989). *Images And Words* (1992) with new singer James LaBrie nailed their character and broke them to the MTV audience with the epic 'Pull Me Under'. *Live At The Marquee* (1993) and *Awake* (1994) consolidated their following. Dream Theater have rarely been complacent, and later releases included *Metropolis Part 2: Scenes From A Memory* (1999), *Six Degrees Of Inner Turbulence*, *Train Of Thought* (2003), *Octavarium* (2005), *Systematic Chaos* (2006) and *Black Clouds & Silver Linings* (2009).

Petrucci's first side project was *Liquid Tension Experiment* (1998) with Portnoy, Rudess and Tony Levin. Its success resulted in *Liquid Tension Experiment 2* (1999). In 2001 Petrucci joined the G3 tour of North America with guitarists Joe Satriani and Steve Vai. He toured again with them in 2005, playing music from his solo album *Suspended Animation* (2005) on his Ernie Ball/Music Man guitars.

**DATE OF BIRTH**

12 July 1967

**PLACE OF BIRTH**

Long Island, USA

**GENRES**

Progressive Metal, Progressive Rock, Jazz Fusion

# PRINCE

## A TALENTED SHOWMAN

Prince Rogers Nelson won a contract with Warner Bros. in 1977 and hit the top of the *Billboard* R&B chart with 'I Wanna Be Your Lover' in 1979, but it was with *1999* (1982) that Prince really consolidated his reputation, giving the world a party song that long outlasted its title date. In 1984, Prince starred in the movie *Purple Rain*, whose soundtrack spent 24 weeks at US No. 1. In 1986 *Parade* spawned the sparse funk of 'Kiss' and served as the soundtrack to the film *Under The Cherry Moon*. He continued his roll with *Sign 'O' The Times* (1987), but *Lovesexy* (1988) was a commercial disaster. In 1991 Prince found new form with the New Power Generation and the hit *Diamonds And Pearls*.

The following year, Prince's twelfth album was released with a cryptic, unpronounceable symbol as its title. During the Act II tour of 1992 he took this 'Love Symbol' as his name and was referred to the Artist Formerly Known As Prince. In 1994 he released the single 'The Most Beautiful Girl In The World' independently, and the song became his biggest hit in years. Prince set up his own label, NPG, and released the albums *Crystal Ball*, *Newpower Soul* and others that didn't excite long-time fans. He resurged, however, with *Musicology* (2004) and was inducted into the Rock And Roll Hall Of Fame in 2004. *LOtUSFLOW3R* (2009) was a return to his guitar-rock past and part of a triple album set that included *MPLSoUND* and Bria Valente's *Elixer*.

### DATE OF BIRTH

7 June 1958

### PLACE OF BIRTH

Minneapolis, USA

### GENRES

Pop, Rock, Funk, R&B

# BONNIE RAITT

## COUNTRY BLUES CLASS

The daughter of vocalist John Raitt and pianist-singer Marge Goddard, young Bonnie was given a Stella guitar as a Christmas present, which her parents insisted she play at family gatherings. She started to play clubs around Boston while at college, supporting blues legends such as Muddy Waters, Son House and John Lee Hooker, and was opening for Mississippi Fred McDowell in New York in 1970 when she landed a contract with Warner. Her debut album, *Bonnie Raitt* (1971), mixed covers of blues standards with her own material. Subsequent albums matched its critical acclaim but sold in modest quantities until she achieved a breakthrough with her version of Del Shannon's 'Runaway' from *Sweet Forgiveness* (1977). Her momentum stalled, however, and she was dropped by Warner in 1983.

Without a record contract for much of the Eighties, Bonnie struggled with alcohol and drugs, but kept touring and remained politically active. After signing to Capitol in 1989, she finally achieved commercial success with three chart-topping albums, *Nick Of Time* (1989), *Luck Of The Draw* (1991) and *Longing In Their Hearts* (1994), which earned her an armful of Grammy awards. Since 1969, Bonnie has used her Fender Stratocaster at every gig, backed up by her signature-model Stratocasters.

### DATE OF BIRTH

8 November 1949

### PLACE OF BIRTH

Burbank, USA

### GENRES

Country, Blues, Blues Rock

# DJANGO REINHARDT

## GYPSY GUITAR GIANT

Gypsy Django Reinhardt made his first recordings with accordionist Jean Vaissade for the Ideal Company. In 1928 his left hand and right side were badly burned in an accident, but he created a whole new fingering system built around the two fingers on his left hand that had full mobility. In 1934 The Quintet Of The Hot Club Of France was formed by a chance meeting of Django and violinist Stéphane Grappelli. They played regularly and filled out with Roger Chaput (guitar), Louis Vola (bass) and eventually Django's brother Joseph (guitar).

The small record company Ultraphone recorded the Hot Club's first sides, 'Dinah', 'Tiger Rag', 'Oh Lady Be Good' and 'I Saw Stars'. These made a big impression, and the Quintet went on to record hundreds of sides. Django also played and recorded with many American jazz legends such as Coleman Hawkins, Benny Carter, Rex Stewart and Louis Armstrong. War broke out while the Quintet was touring in England and Django returned to Paris while Grappelli remained in England, but they reunited after the war. He toured briefly with Duke Ellington in America and returned to Paris, where he finally retired in 1951, sadly dying from a brain haemorrhage two years later.

### DATE OF BIRTH/DEATH

23 January 1910/16 May 1953

### PLACE OF BIRTH

Liberchies, Belgium

### GENRES

Romany, Continental Jazz

# JOHN RENBOURN

## FATHER OF MODERN FOLK

John Renbourn's first love was skiffle, but he later turned to folk music. In 1966 he was playing folk music in Soho where he met many other musicians, including Paul Simon, Davey Graham and Bert Jansch. Renbourn and Jansch both had fledgling recording careers at the time and Renbourn performed on Jansch's second album. Afterwards they teamed up formally to record *Bert And John* (1966). They developed an intricate duet style that became known as 'folk baroque'.

In 1967 the two founded Pentangle and remained together until 1978. Renbourn continued to release such solo albums as *The Hermit* (1976) and *The Black Balloon* (1979). He formed the John Renbourn Group in the Eighties and began adding East Indian percussion and jazz woodwinds to his music. He then teamed up with guitarist Stefan Grossman and embarked upon a series of world tours. They recorded a few albums before Renbourn went on to found the ensemble Ship Of Fools and play music with a stronger Celtic influence. He continues to tour alone and with other guitarists. He also occasionally reunites with Jansch and in 2005 he collaborated with Clive Carroll on the score for the film *Driving Lessons*.

### DATE OF BIRTH

8 August 1944

### PLACE OF BIRTH

London, England

### GENRES

Folk, Classical, Blues, World

# RANDY RHOADS

## QUIET RIOT TO OZZY

William Randall 'Randy' Rhoads grew up with a strong musical background and played in various bands from the age of 14. He formed Quiet Riot in 1976 with friend and bassist Kelly Garni and vocalist Kevin DuBrow. They gained a strong following in LA, but were unable to get a US record deal, signing instead with Columbia in Japan. Neither *Quiet Riot* (1977) nor *Quiet Riot II* (1978) was released in America. In 1979 Rhoads successfully auditioned for Ozzy Osbourne, who was recruiting a new band, and came to the UK to record *Blizzard Of Ozz* (1980). Rhoads co-wrote seven tracks, including 'Mr Crowley' with its neo-classical guitar solo.

The band toured Britain, where the album went Top 10, and then hurriedly recorded a second album, *Diary Of A Madman* (1981), with Rhoads co-writing every track including 'Flying High Again', on which his compact solo ushered in a new style of Eighties metal guitar. The band played a five-month US tour during the summer of 1981 and commenced another four-month schedule at the end of the year as sales of both albums took off. Rhoads was killed in a plane crash in 1982, and a live album, *Tribute*, was released in 1987.

**DATE OF BIRTH/DEATH**

6 December 1956/19 March 1982

**PLACE OF BIRTH**

Santa Monica, USA

**GENRES**

Heavy Metal, Hard Rock

# KEITH RICHARDS
## ICON OF EXCESS

Veteran guitarist Keith Richards developed a passion for music as a teenager. In 1962 he successfully auditioned for Brian Jones's rhythm and blues outfit, which would ultimately evolve into The Rolling Stones. The recruitment of Mick Jagger (vocals) Bill Wyman (bass) and Charlie Watts (drums) completed the line-up, but the foundations were laid by Richards and Jones spending time trying to figure out how bluesmen such as Robert Johnson and Muddy Waters achieved their sounds. Their interlocking lead and rhythm guitars can be heard to good effect on *Rolling Stones* (1964), *Rolling Stones No. 2* (1965) and *Out Of Our Heads* (1965), but Richards was at his creative best on *Beggars Banquet* (1968), playing all the guitar parts on the album. After Jones's departure in 1968, Richards combined effortlessly with replacement guitarist Mick Taylor, and later still with Ronnie Wood.

At times almost as famous for his intake of narcotics as his musical ability, Richards is an innovative player, claiming the first chart hit to feature a fuzzbox,'(I Can't Get No) Satisfaction', while his use of open tunings became a trademark. He was often associated with the Fender Telecaster, but in recent years he has favoured the Gibson ES-345.

**DATE OF BIRTH**

18 December 1943

**PLACE OF BIRTH**

Dartford, England

**GENRES**

Rock, Blues, Country, Reggae, R&B

# LEE RITENOUR

## CAPTAIN FINGERS

Lee Ritenour began his career as a session player at 16. He played his first recording session with The Mamas & the Papas in 1968 and, by the mid–Seventies, was a much sought–after session guitarist. In 1976 Ritenour released his first solo album, *First Course*. This was followed up by his fusion work *Captain Fingers* in 1976. Since *First Course* he has released over 30 albums, including *Rit's House* in 2002. One of his most notable works is his pop album *Rit* (1981), which featured vocalist Eric Tagg and contained the chart hits 'Is It You' and 'Mr Briefcase'. In the Nineties, he was one of the founding members of group Fourplay. In February 2004 Ritenour completed a project looking back on his career called *Overtime*, and he released *Smoke n' Mirrors*, which featured his 13–year–old son, in 2006.

In the early Eighties Ritenour was given his own Ibanez signature–model guitar, the LR–10, which can be heard exclusively on his album *Rit*. Currently Ritenour plays the Gibson ES–335 and L5 that he first played in the Seventies, and also plays his signature Lee Ritenour Model archtop made by Gibson.

### DATE OF BIRTH

11 January 1952

### PLACE OF BIRTH

Los Angeles, USA

### GENRES

Rock, Pop

# NILE RODGERS
## THE FUNKY CRAFTSMAN

Nile Rodgers played with the Sesame Street band in his teens, and then worked in the house band at Harlem's Apollo Theater. He met Bernard Edwards in 1970 and they formed a rock band called The Boys (later The Big Apple Band), but couldn't land a record deal. In 1977 they joined forces with drummer Tony Thompson to form the funk/R&B band Chic. The band scored numerous Top 10 hits, including 'Everybody Dance', 'Le Freak' and 'Good Times', and helped propel the disco craze. The band's sound turned Rodgers and Edwards into coveted producers and an early success came with the group Sister Sledge. In 1980 the team produced Diana Ross's album *Diana*. Then, in 1983, Rodgers produced David Bowie's album *Let's Dance*, and in 1984 helmed Madonna's blockbuster album *Like A Virgin*. Duran Duran worked extensively with Rodgers after he produced the hit single 'The Reflex' (1983).

Rodgers and Edwards reunited Chic in the Nineties for a successful tour but, in 1996, while on a tour of Japan, his partner Edwards died of pneumonia. Rodgers later formed a music distribution company and headed several efforts on behalf of victims of the 2001 terrorist attacks.

**DATE OF BIRTH**

19 September 1952

**PLACE OF BIRTH**

New York, USA

**GENRES**

Funk, Pop, R&B

# MICK RONSON

## BOWIE'S BACKING

Mick Ronson played in local bands throughout the mid–Sixties in his native Hull and endured a failed stint trying to establish himself in London before joining The Rats. In 1970 former Rat John Cambridge recruited Ronson for David Bowie's backup band. The band, originally called The Hype, at points included producer Tony Visconti and keyboardist Rick Wakeman. Ronson's flair for arranging and playing grounded Bowie as he developed his outsized persona on early albums such as *The Man Who Sold the World* (1970) and *The Rise And Fall Of Ziggy Stardust And The Spiders From Mars* (1972).

Ronson's playing and arranging brought him the producer's hat in 1972 for Lou Reed's *Transformer* with Bowie, as well as the unlikely leap to work on American country–rock group Pure Prairie League's *Bustin' Out* (1972). Ronson played on Bowie's *Aladdin Sane* and *Pin Ups* (both 1973), but left Bowie after the 'Farewell Concert' in 1973. In the ensuing years Ronson released three solo albums. The first, *Slaughter On 10th Avenue* (1974), featured Ronson's best–known solo piece, 'Only After Dark'. After a stint with Mott The Hoople, Ronson worked with former Hoople singer Ian Hunter. His last high–profile live performance was his appearance at The Freddie Mercury Tribute Concert in 1992, before tragically dying of liver cancer the following year.

### DATE OF BIRTH/DEATH

26 May 1946/29 April 1993

### PLACE OF BIRTH

Hull, England

### GENRES

Rock, Glam Rock

# FRANCIS ROSSI & RICK PARFITT

## MORE THAN THE STATUS QUO

Francis Rossi (pictured right) and Rick Parfitt (pictured left) struck up a friendship in 1965, when Rossi was already playing in an early incarnation of Status Quo. Parfitt was invited to join as rhythm guitarist shortly before the fashionably psychedelic 'Pictures Of Matchstick Men' became their first British (and only American) hit early in 1968. Two years later, the single 'Down The Dustpipe' heralded an abrupt change of direction and third album *Ma Kelly's Greasy Spoon* (1970) confirmed that Quo had swapped psychedelia for 12–bar boogie. As the Seventies progressed, Quo honed their accessible hard rock, finding mainstream acceptance via a string of hit singles and well–received albums.

Shortly before famously opening Live Aid in London with 'Rockin' All Over The World' in July 1985, Quo had apparently retired, but the Wembley gig proved the catalyst for reformation and the band remained active. Although singles such as 'Living On An Island' and 'In The Army Now' amply demonstrated their versatility, Rossi and Parfitt relish playing up to the cartoon image of Quo, as the title of their 2007 album, *In Search Of The Fourth Chord*, attests. Status Quo command a substantial following in Europe and have chalked up more hit singles in Britain than any other act, becoming a national treasure in the process. Francis Rossi's debut solo album, *One Step At A Time*, was released in 2010.

### DATE OF BIRTH
Rossi: 29 May 1949/Parfitt: 12 October 1948

### PLACE OF BIRTH
Rossi: London, England/Parfitt: Woking, England

### GENRES
Rock'n'Roll, Hard Rock

# ULI JON ROTH
## SCORPIONS TO SKY GUITAR

From 1973 to 1978, Uli Jon Roth was the songwriter and lead guitarist for legendary German rock group The Scorpions. Roth recorded five albums with the band, the final one being 1978's *Taken By Force*, which featured the Roth-penned 'Sails Of Charon'. This track, which Roth says was musically inspired by a Tchaikovsky violin concerto, represents arguably the first example of neo-classical shred guitar. Soon after, though, Roth left The Scorpions and formed Electric Sun, which lasted until 1985. During this time Roth focused more on the neo-classical aspects of his guitar playing. To execute his classically based compositional ideas, he replaced his beloved Fender Strat with a six-octave 32-fret guitar. The result, the Sky Guitar, made its debut on Electric Sun's final album, *Beyond The Astral Skies* (1984).

Starting in 1985, Roth spent much of his time working in the classical music spectrum, writing four symphonies and two concertos, and playing with symphony orchestras throughout Europe. In 1998, however, he stepped back on to the big rock stage for the European leg of the G3 tour. In 2000 he released the two-disc set *Transcendental Sky Guitar* and, in 2004, the concerto *Metamorphosis Of Vivaldi's Four Seasons*, a twenty-first century incarnation of the spirit of Vivaldi's music. His *Under A Dark Sky* album was released in Japan in 2008.

**DATE OF BIRTH**

18 December 1954

**PLACE OF BIRTH**

Düsseldorf, Germany

**GENRES**

Hard Rock, Classical, Heavy Metal

# TODD RUNDGREN
## FROM ECLECTIC TO ICONIC

Perhaps no other artist has forged so eclectic a career as guitarist–singer–songwriter–producer–technologist–experimenter Todd Rundgren. In his 40 years on the rock scene, Rundgren has pursued interests ranging from pop songcraft to experimental composition, and from innovative record production to nostalgic reinvention tours. He began playing in bar bands, culminating in Woody's Truck Stop. In 1967 he left to form The Nazz, which landed a record deal in 1968, and the debut album's first single was a slow version of Rundgren's later hit, 'Hello, It's Me'. Rundgren left to record independently, using the name 'Runt' in his album titles – this arguably being the name of the new 'band', which initially featured brothers Hunt and Tony Sales, or, more accurately, an alter ego that served as a front for his expanding solo skills. The first album generated a buzz in 1971 with the Top 40 hit 'We Gotta Get You A Woman'. At the same time, Rundgren became an in-demand producer, helming The Band's *Stage Fright* (1970) and Badfinger's *Straight Up* (1971).

Rundgren's third solo album, *Something/Anything?* (1972) became a smash because of the Carole King tribute, 'I Saw the Light', and the reworked 'Hello, It's Me'. But Rundgren, proclaiming his disinterest in being a pop star, followed up in 1973 with *A Wizard, A True Star*, which turned off the mainstream audience. Rundgren later experimented with glam and prog rock and expanded his production skills into computer–based, commercial video operations.

### DATE OF BIRTH

22 June 1948

### PLACE OF BIRTH

Upper Darby, USA

### GENRES

Rock, Progressive Rock, Hard Rock, Pop

# RICHIE SAMBORA

## A GUITAR HERO AMONG US

Richard Stephen 'Richie' Sambora began playing guitar in his early teens, inspired by Jimi Hendrix, Eric Clapton, Jeff Beck and The Beatles. In 1978, he made his recording debut with his band Shark Frenzy, but the mix tapes were damaged in a flood and never saw the light of day. In 1983, Jon Bongiovi hired Sambora to replace guitarist Dave Sabo in his newly signed band Bon Jovi. The rest, as they say, is history. Over the past 25 years, Bon Jovi has released 10 studio albums that have sold over 120 million copies, and the band has played over 2,500 shows in over 50 countries. Sambora has released two critically acclaimed solo albums – *Stranger In This Town* (1991) and *Undiscovered Soul* (1998). Few guitarists have spent as much time onstage as Sambora has in his remarkable career.

Through the years, Sambora has played just about every guitar possible. In the early years of Bon Jovi, he favoured custom Gibson Les Pauls, but then went through a period of 'super–Strats', from such manufacturers as Charvel, Jackson and Kramer, the latter of which made his first signature model guitar, in 1987. Since then, the guitarist has continued to mix it up and in 2008 Sambora announced his new ESP endorsement deal, before Bon Jovi released *The Circle* the following year.

**DATE OF BIRTH**

11 July 1959

**PLACE OF BIRTH**

Perth Amboy, USA

**GENRES**

Rock, Hard Rock, Glam Rock

# CARLOS SANTANA

## SANTANA'S SEARING COLOSSUS

The Santana Blues Band was formed in 1966, incorporating the Afro–Cuban rhythms of Latin America, which complemented Santana's lyrical guitar style. Carlos made his first appearance on record as a guest on *The Live Adventures Of Mike Bloomfield And Al Kooper* (1968), produced by Bill Graham. Graham pulled off a remarkable coup in securing Santana a slot at the Woodstock Festival in August 1969, which proved their turning point. The recruitment of Neal Schon gave the band a harder–edged dual–guitar sound for *Santana III* (1971). *Caravanserai* (1972) introduced various new musicians and veered into jazz–rock fusion territory. Further excursions in this direction in the mid–Seventies saw Santana's commercial fortunes start to decline and Graham encouraged Santana to adopt a more chart–friendly approach. The guitarist obliged with *Amigos* (1976). By returning to the Latin feel and adding a dose of funk, Santana arrived at a formula that would serve him for several years to come.

The Nineties were a low point, but Santana pulled off a remarkable comeback by assembling an all–star cast for *Supernatural* (1999), which won nine Grammy Awards. It was followed by *Shaman* (2003) *and All That I Am* (2005), which mixed hip hop and pop with Santana's familiar lyrical Latin guitar.

### DATE OF BIRTH

20 July 1947

### PLACE OF BIRTH

Autlán de Navarro, Mexico

### GENRES

Rock, Jazz Rock, Latin, Funk, Hip Hop, Pop

# JOEY SANTIAGO

## THE FORCE BEHIND PIXIES

Joey Santiago first played guitar at the age of nine, becoming a fan of Seventies punk and David Bowie. At the University of Massachusetts, he met Black Francis (Charles Thompson) and they formed a band in 1985. Bassist Kim Deal was recruited via a telling advertisement seeking someone who was into Peter, Paul & Mary and Hüsker Dü. Drummer David Lovering completed the line-up, which became Pixies.

Securing a contract with British independent 4AD, Pixies debuted with the mini-album *Come On Pilgrim* (1987), which established their powerful, guitar-driven sound. Santiago's innovative, angular lead was evident on 'Holiday Song' and 'Vamos'. Their first full-length album *Surfer Rosa* (1988) was heavy and frenzied, while *Doolittle* (1989) was less raw and included some of their best-known songs, the poppy 'Here Comes Your Man' and ferocious opener 'Un Chien Andalou'. After two more albums, the Pixies fell prey to internal tensions and disbanded in 1993. Santiago maintained a good relationship with Francis, now known as Frank Black, and contributed lead guitar to several of his solo albums. He formed The Martinis with wife Linda Mallari, but only recorded one song in the Nineties. Their debut album *Smitten* belatedly emerged in 2004, the same year that Pixies reformed for an ongoing tour, though only one new song, 'Bam Thwok' (2004), has been released.

**DATE OF BIRTH**

10 June 1965

**PLACE OF BIRTH**

Manila, Philippines

**GENRES**

Alternative Rock

A-Z OF
GUITAR GODS

# JOE SATRIANI

## GUITAR GIANT

American guitarist Joe Satriani is widely credited with pioneering the rock-instrumental style in the Eighties. By the age of 17 he was giving guitar lessons to students, including classmate Steve Vai. In 1986 he released his first, self-financed album, *Not Of This Earth*, focusing on sound textures rather than technique. *Surfing With The Alien* (1987) was his major breakthrough, highlighting his composing, production and playing talents. *Flying In A Blue Dream* (1989) had a more experimental feel, exploring harmony and counterpoint and displaying a sense of humour on 'The Phone Call'. *The Extremist* (1992) put more emphasis on melodic rock.

In 1993 Satriani joined Deep Purple when Ritchie Blackmore quit the band in the middle of a tour, but he turned down the offer to join them permanently. *Time Machine* (1993) consisted of studio tracks from earlier EPs together with recent live material, while *Joe Satriani* (1995), took a more relaxed, bluesier approach. In 1996 Satriani set up the first G3 tour of North America with Vai and Eric Johnson, and it became a regular event. Meanwhile Satriani continued his own career with *Crystal Planet* (1998), *Engines Of Creation* (2000), *Strange Beautiful Music* (2002), *Is There Love In Space?* (2004) and *Super Colossal* (2006). In 2009 he released Chickenfoot's self-titled debut album, recorded with Chili Peppers drummer Chad Smith and Van Halen's Sammy Hagar and Michael Anthony.

### DATE OF BIRTH

15 July 1958

### PLACE OF BIRTH

Westbury, USA

### GENRES

Hard Rock, Instrumental Rock, Jazz Fusion

# MICHAEL SCHENKER

## UFO GUITAR LEGEND

Michael Schenker was first turned on to the guitar when his older brother Rudolf brought home a Gibson Flying V. Inspired by Hank Marvin and Mountain's Leslie West, Michael taught himself to play and joined Rudolf in The Scorpions, recording their first album, *Lonesome Crow* (1972), when he was just 17. During the ensuing tour, British space–metal group UFO witnessed Schenker's guitar chops and asked him to join the band. Michael took the gig. His first album with UFO, *Phenomenon* (1974), contained such future hard–rock classics as 'Doctor Doctor' and 'Rock Bottom'. The album also contained an instrumental track titled 'Lipstick Traces', which Schenker played entirely with his feet.

After several more successful albums, in 1979 Schenker's alcohol abuse caused his exit from UFO. He rejoined The Scorpions, staying just long enough to record *Lovedrive* (1979). Following this, he set out on his own, starting the first of many incarnations of the Michael Schenker Group (MSG). Craving commercial success, however, he steered away from his hard–rock roots, and came to the cusp with singer Robin McCauley supplying the 'M' in MSG. Since then, Schenker has focused mostly on solo albums, including three releases in 2001 alone (*MS 2000: Dreams And Expressions*, *Odd Trio* and *Be Aware Of Scorpions*), while he continues to tour with MSG.

### DATE OF BIRTH

10 January 1955

### PLACE OF BIRTH

Sarstedt, Germany

### GENRES

Hard Rock, Heavy Metal

# NEAL SCHON

## JOURNEY'S SOUL

Rock and jazz guitarist Neal Schon was the son of a jazz saxophonist and composer. A precocious talent, he learned guitar at the age of 10 and joined Santana at 15. Schon made two albums with the band, *Santana III* (1971) and *Caravanserai* (1972). In 1972, he played with Azteca, a Latin jazz–rock fusion ensemble. In 1973, Schon formed Journey with former Santana band member Greg Rolie on keyboards and vocals. Signed to Columbia Records, the debut album *Journey* (1975) and the follow-ups *Look Into The Future* (1976) and *Next* (1977) were all firmly in the jazz–rock mould, featuring long tracks and lengthy instrumental workouts. The albums sold poorly, prompting a change in direction on *Infinity* (1978) to a pomp–rock sound similar to Boston and Foreigner.

This marked the start of a run of success for Journey that would bring them to a whole new audience, peaking with their best-selling work *Escape* (1981). Schon also recorded two albums with keyboardist Jan Hammer and has issued sporadic solo recordings since. After Journey split, he joined forces with former Baby's singer John Waite in Bad English in 1988. A reformed Journey released *Trial By Fire* in 1996 and, various new singers down the line, *Revelation* in 2008.

**DATE OF BIRTH**

27 February 1954

**PLACE OF BIRTH**

Oklahoma City, USA

**GENRES**

Hard Rock, Jazz Rock

# JOHN SCOFIELD

## A JAZZ-GUITAR GREAT

After making his recording debut with Gerry Mulligan and Chet Baker, John Scofield was a member of the Billy Cobham/George Duke band for two years. In 1977 he recorded with Charles Mingus and then joined Gary Burton's quartet. That same year, Scofield released his debut solo album, titled simply *John Scofield*, beginning his career as a bandleader. In 1979 the guitarist teamed up with his mentor Steve Swallow and drummer Andy Nussbaum to form The John Scofield Trio. From 1982 to 1985, Scofield toured and recorded with Miles Davis. Since that time, Scofield has prominently led his trio and other groups in the international jazz scene, recording over 30 albums as a leader, including collaborations with Pat Metheny, Charlie Haden, Medeski, Bill Frisell, Brad Mehldau, Joe Lovano and Phil Lesh. He has also played and recorded with many jazz legends, including Jim Hall, Ron Carter and Herbie Hancock, among others. Recent highlights include his excursions into the drum'n'bass electronic music world on 2002's *Überjam*, as well as the more traditional sounds of *Saudades* (2006).

For nearly 20 years Scofield has plied his lines on an Ibanez AS-200 and, more recently, on his signature-model Ibanez JSM100, through a Mesa/Boogie Mark I reissue and an arsenal of modulation effects.

### DATE OF BIRTH

26 December 1951

### PLACE OF BIRTH

Dayton, USA

### GENRES

Contemporary Jazz, Jazz Funk, Jazz Fusion

# ANDRÉS SEGOVIA

## A CLASSICAL LEGEND

Classical-guitar legend Andrés Segovia taught himself to play guitar, developing his own style and technique. Segovia plucked the strings with a combination of his fingernails and fingertips, producing a sharper sound than many of his contemporaries. As his talent developed, his reputation spread and, in 1909, he made his public debut. By 1919 Segovia was ready for a fully fledged tour, and performed in that year in South America, where he gained an enthusiastic reception. Still, there was a limited repertoire for guitar, and so Segovia transcribed works written for other instruments. He relied primarily on Renaissance and Baroque pieces composed for lute or Spanish vihuela. In Germany he discovered the lute works of Sylvius Leopold Weiss, which were adaptable and effective. He also discovered a group of Bach's works that were well suited to the guitar.

The outbreak of the Spanish Civil War forced Segovia to leave Spain in 1936. He toured extensively in Central and South America before returning to the United States in 1943. Over the next 20 years, through worldwide performances and with the help of the new medium of television, Segovia secured his place as the pre-eminent classical guitarist of the modern age. He died of a heart attack, aged 94.

### DATE OF BIRTH/DEATH

21 February 1893/2 June 1987

### PLACE OF BIRTH

Linares, Spain

### GENRES

Classical

A-Z OF
GUITAR GODS

# KEVIN SHIELDS

## MY BLOODY GENIUS

Kevin Shields was born in Queens, New York City, but moved to Dublin, Ireland, at age 10, where he learned guitar. My Bloody Valentine came together in 1984. The band moved to Holland and then Berlin, where they recorded the mini–album *This Is Your Bloody Valentine* (1985). They reconvened in London the following year, going on to make three EPs. With Bilinda Butcher recruited as main vocalist, they made other recordings, and finally signed to Creation Records in 1988. The band produced 'You Made Me Realise', an EP that brought them to wider attention and acclaim. They followed up with *Isn't Anything* (1988), which defined My Bloody Valentine's idiosyncratic approach. Shields' onslaught of meticulously layered guitars was demonstrated on the single 'Feed Me With Your Kiss'. Shields was a perfectionist in the studio, painstakingly assembling *Loveless* (1991), which consolidated their position as a leading indie band and inspired outfits such as Ride, Chapterhouse, Slowdive and the short–lived shoe–gazing trend. It proved to be the last My Bloody Valentine album to date. Shields has continued to work as a producer and remixer.

Shields has customized the tremolo arms of his Fender Jaguar and Jazzmaster guitars to achieve his trademark sound. The warped effect this produced caused some buyers of *Loveless* to return their vinyl copies.

### DATE OF BIRTH
21 May 1963

### PLACE OF BIRTH
New York, USA

### GENRES
Alternative Rock

# ALEX SKOLNICK

## TESTAMENT TO A PIONEER

Alex Skolnick is best known as a metal guitarist with thrash pioneers Testament. But metal is just one facet of the talented guitarist's abilities. Skolnick joined a band called Legacy at age 16. Two years later, the band changed their name to Testament and released *The Legacy* in 1987. Five more albums followed before Skolnick disbanded in 1992. During that era Skolnick saw one of Miles Davis's guitar-driven bands on television, sparking an intense passion for jazz music. While studying for his degree in jazz performance he founded the Alex Skolnick Trio. Their first recording, *Goodbye To Romance: Standards For A New Generation* (2002), featured jazz arrangements of classic metal songs. Subsequent releases *Transformation* (2004) and *Last Day In Paradise* (2007) featured similar work.

In recent years, Skolnick has toured as a member of the Trans-Siberian Orchestra, a classical-rock odyssey that performs technically demanding arrangements of Christmas songs to sold-out arenas. He is also featured in Jekyll & Hyde In Concert, the touring version of the hit Broadway show *Jekyll & Hyde*, and has begun working with composer Jim Steinman on the Dream Engine project, performing new songs and classics. In 2005, Skolnick reunited with Testament for a tour of Europe and Japan, and their new album is due in 2010.

### DATE OF BIRTH

29 September 1968

### PLACE OF BIRTH

Berkeley, USA

### GENRES

Heavy Metal, Thrash Metal, Jazz

# SLASH

## APPETITE FOR BRILLIANCE

The man beneath the top hat, Saul 'Slash' Hudson was born in London but grew up in Los Angeles where, at the age of 14, he heard Aerosmith's *Rocks* and found his life's calling. Practising guitar for hours on end, Slash set about forming his own band Road Crew with friend and drummer Steven Adler. Soon they hooked up with singer Axl Rose, guitarist Izzy Stradlin and bassist Duff McKagan to form a new band called Guns N' Roses. In 1987, GN'R released its debut, *Appetite For Destruction*, which became one of the biggest hard rock albums in history. On an individual level, it established Slash as the era's premier guitar anti-hero. His meteoric ascension impacted the guitar-gear world, restoring the once grand but then-stalled Gibson brand to its prior position of esteem.

Following the demise of GN'R, Slash released two albums with Slash's Snakepit and recorded sessions with dozens of top-name artists. Then, in 2003, he reunited with former Gunners McKagan and Matt Sorum and recruited guitarist Dave Kushner and former Stone Temple Pilots singer Scott Weiland to form Velvet Revolver. The band's two releases, *Contraband* (2004) and *Libertad* (2007), along with a self-titled solo album of 2010, have helped to return Slash to the world's biggest stages and positioned him as one of the enduring guitar heroes of his generation.

**DATE OF BIRTH**

23 July 1965

**PLACE OF BIRTH**

London, England

**GENRES**

Hard Rock

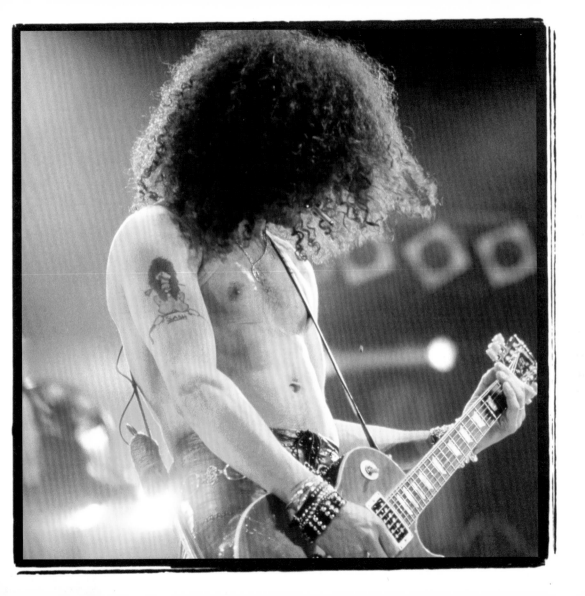

# ADRIAN SMITH

## IRON MAIDEN TO ICON

At school, Adrian Smith was drawn to the rock–guitar sounds of Jimi Hendrix and Ritchie Blackmore, and so set about learning how to play. He became friends with Dave Murray and formed Urchin, but Murray soon left to form Iron Maiden. Urchin fell apart, so Smith welcomed the invitation to once again play alongside Murray in 1981. Starting with *Killers* (1981), and continuing with *Number Of The Beast* (1982), *Piece Of Mind* (1983), *Powerslave* (1984), *Somewhere In Time* (1986) and *Seventh Son Of A Seventh Son* (1988), Smith's deceptively 'lazy' and melodic soloing played perfect straight man to Murray's often fiery, scalar lines.

Equally important to Maiden's sound and success was Smith's songwriting sensibilities. He wrote or co–wrote such hits as 'Flight Of Icarus', '2 Minutes To Midnight' and 'Can I Play With Madness', and helped steer the band into ever more progressive waters. This direction, however, collided with bassist Steve Harris's musical vision and Smith left to pursue solo ambitions. Recording under the acronym A.S.A.P. (Adrian Smith And Project), he released *Silver And Gold* (1989) and later formed the alternative rock–influenced Psycho Motel, releasing *State Of Mind* (1996) and *Welcome To The World* (1997). Smith rejoined Maiden in 1999 and continues to record and tour with them, most recently on their 2010 *The Final Frontier* album and tour.

**DATE OF BIRTH**

27 February 1957

**PLACE OF BIRTH**

London, England

**GENRES**

Heavy Metal, Hard Rock

A–Z OF
GUITAR GODS

# STEVE STEVENS

## BILLY IDOL TO GUITAR IDOL

Brooklyn's Steve Stevens grew up as a fan of progressive rock and studied guitar at LaGuardia High School of Performing Arts. He worked the Long Island and Manhattan club scenes with bands and eventually was hired for session work, including tracks for ex–Kiss drummer Peter Criss. But Stevens' star really began to shine when he met Billy Idol. With Stevens' flamboyant shredding jumping out of his songs and videos, Idol's new solo works became smashes. Stevens' connection with Idol led to work with Michael Jackson (*Bad*), Ric Ocasek (*This Side Of Paradise*), Thompson Twins (*Here's To Future Days*) and Robert Palmer (*Don't Explain*). From 1992 to 1994 Stevens worked with ex–Mötley Crüe singer Vince Neil on the album *Exposed*.

Stevens eventually got back to his prog–rock roots, working with bassist Tony Levin and drummer Terry Bozzio in the Bozzio Levin Stevens group, recording 1997's *Black Light Syndrome* and 2000's *Situation Dangerous*. Stevens reunited with Idol in 1999 for a series of tours. They appeared in 2002 in an episode of 'VH1 Storytellers'. Stevens also appeared in the Billy Idol episode of VH1's 'Behind The Music'. Stevens, influenced by the great flamenco guitarist Paco de Lucía, also recorded a solo release, *Flamenco A Go-Go* (1999).

### DATE OF BIRTH

5 May 1959

### PLACE OF BIRTH

New York, USA

### GENRES

Hard Rock, Progressive Rock, New Wave, Instrumental Rock

# STEPHEN STILLS

## CROSBY, STAR AND NASH

An oft-travelled military child, Stills gravitated to California in 1965 after stints with New York-based groups the Au Go Go Singers, which included singer Richie Furay, and The Company, a folk-rock group that toured Canada, where Stills met Squires guitarist Neil Young. In California Stills recruited Furay and Young to form Buffalo Springfield and made his first international splash with the socially conscious 'For What It's Worth' (1967). A jam session at the home of Joni Mitchell united Stills and former Byrd David Crosby with singer Graham Nash. As Crosby, Stills & Nash, the trio made a landmark appearance at Woodstock in 1969, and their eponymous debut album became an international smash. The band added Neil Young for the second album *Déjà Vu* (1970), and have continued to perform together in various combinations into the twenty-first century.

Along the way Stills branched off with projects such as his band Manassas, which produced three albums, the first being self-titled, on which he demonstrated his songwriting mastery in hard rock and Latin genres as well as acoustic and country rock. Stills' first two solo albums spawned the hits 'Love the One You're With' and 'Change Partners' (both 1970). As a guitarist Stills was notorious for wild experimentation, and CSNY's sound is identifiable for its rich acoustic guitars. Stills is currently reissuing his Manassas recordings, and underwent his first solo tour in 2008.

**DATE OF BIRTH**

3 January 1945

**PLACE OF BIRTH**

Dallas, USA

**GENRES**

Folk Rock, Blues Rock, Country Rock, Hard Rock, Latin

A-Z OF GUITAR GODS

# ANDY SUMMERS

## AUTHORITY OF THE POLICE

Andrew 'Andy' Summers started out in Zoot Money's Big Roll Band, a jazzy soul and R&B outfit that became a regular fixture on London's Soho scene. After studying in America, he returned home and worked as a session guitarist before landing a job as sideman for Neil Sedaka, a gig he got through guitarist Robert Fripp. In 1977, a chance meeting with drummer Stewart Copeland led to him joining the short-lived Strontium 90 with Copeland, vocalist Mike Howlett and bassist Sting. Copeland and Sting then invited Summers to join The Police. Their debut album *Outlandos d'Amour* (1978) brought the band's unique brand of jazz- and reggae-influenced punk-pop to worldwide prominence. In 1983 the trio released *Synchronicity*, which topped the *Billboard* charts and spawned the No. 1 smash 'Every Breath You Take'. But just as the band reached the pinnacle of pop music, it imploded.

After the break-up of The Police, Summers embarked on a solo career, including two instrumental progressive-rock albums, *I Advance Masked* (1982) and *Bewitched* (1984), with Fripp. He followed with *The Golden Wire* (1989) and *The Last Dance Of Mr X* (1997). Fans hopeful for a reunion eventually got their wish in 2007, while Summers continued to expand his sonic palette with the likes of *Splendid Brasil* (2005) in collaboration with Victor Biglione.

**DATE OF BIRTH**

31 December 1942

**PLACE OF BIRTH**

Poulton-le-Fylde, England

**GENRES**

Rock, Jazz, New Wave, Reggae

# BERNARD SUMNER

## RIDING THE NEW WAVE

New-wave guitarist Bernard Sumner saw Sex Pistols in Manchester in 1976 and was inspired to take up the guitar. Originally called Warsaw, later Joy Division, he and friend Peter Hook recruited Stephen Morris and Ian Curtis and joined local independent label Factory. In-house producer Martin Hannett transformed Joy Division from an ordinary punk outfit into one of the most influential groups of all time. The debut *Unknown Pleasures* (1979) was edgy and atmospheric, Sumner's understated guitar adding texture and leaving space rather than seeking to dominate.

*Closer* (1980) refined their sound into a more stately affair, but shortly before its release, Curtis committed suicide. The others continued as New Order, adding Gillian Gilbert on keyboards, which gave the band a more electronic edge. Their debut album *Movement* (1981) saw Sumner emerge as lead singer and lyricist. *Power, Corruption And Lies* (1982) first showcased the pioneering crossover between dance, electronic music and rock that became their enduring trademark. Their seventh album *Get Ready* (2001) returned the band to guitar-based rock, while 2005's *Waiting For The Sirens' Call* seems to be the original members' final line-up, following Peter Hook's departure in 2007. Sumner favoured a Gibson SG Standard (without vibrola) and also used a Shergold Masquerader and a Vox Phantom.

**DATE OF BIRTH**

4 January 1956

**PLACE OF BIRTH**

Manchester, England

**GENRES**

New Wave

# MICK TAYLOR

## BLUESBREAKING STONE

A guitarist from the age of nine, Mick Taylor was in his teens when he formed a group that subsequently evolved into The Gods. When Eric Clapton failed to turn up for a Bluesbreakers' gig, the 16-year-old Taylor stood in for the second half of the set. When Peter Green left The Bluesbreakers in 1967, Mayall signed Taylor as his replacement. He became known for a style that is based on the blues with overtones of Latin and jazz, attributes that made him ideally qualified to replace Brian Jones in The Rolling Stones. On Taylor's first full album with the Stones, *Sticky Fingers* (1971), he worked with Mick Jagger on 'Moonlight Mile' and 'Sway'. The classic *Exile On Main Street* (1972) featured Taylor and Richards' guitar interplay at its peak. He left the Stones in 1974, convinced that the band was about to collapse.

Taylor's first solo work was the largely overlooked blues and jazz-tinged album *Mick Taylor* (1978). He spent much of the Eighties battling heroin addiction and guested for Bob Dylan and Mark Knopfler. In 2007 he toured as part of the Experience Hendrix tribute group. Taylor is usually associated with the Gibson Les Paul. He used a Gibson ES-355 for *Sticky Fingers* and *Exile On Main Street*, a Gibson SG on tour and, on occasion, a Fender Stratocaster and Telecaster.

**DATE OF BIRTH**

17 January 1949

**PLACE OF BIRTH**

Hatfield, England

**GENRES**

Rock, Blues Rock

# KIM THAYIL

## ONE OF GRUNGE'S GREATS

Grunge guitarist Kim Thayil was inspired to play guitar by Kiss. He bought his first guitar, a Guild S-100, and formed his first band in high school. He became a member of Soundgarden in 1984. Their first album, *Ultramega OK* (1988), was released on independent label SST before they became the first band from the Seattle scene to sign with a major. They released four albums, *Louder Than Love* (1989), *Badmotorfinger* (1991), *Superunknown* (1994) and *Down On The Upside* (1996). Their breakthrough came with *Superunknown*, which featured the singles 'Spoonman' and 'Black Hole Sun'. The final album, *Down On The Upside*, represented a departure from their grunge roots and creative tensions between Thayil and singer Chris Cornell led to a split in 1997. Thayil has since collaborated with former Nirvana bassist Krist Novoselic, The Dead Kennedys' Jello Biafra, Presidents Of The USA and Johnny Cash, and is currently part of the band Set & Setting.

In addition to his Guild S-100, Thayil has also used Gibson Les Paul models, the Gibson Firebird and the Fender Telecaster and Jazzmaster. Along with the apparently accidental use of unusual time signatures, Thayil often employed alternative and unorthodox tunings, 'Black Hole Sun' being performed in a Drop-D tuning.

### DATE OF BIRTH

4 September 1960

### PLACE OF BIRTH

Seattle, USA

### GENRES

Heavy Metal, Alternative Metal, Grunge

# RICHARD THOMPSON

## LAUDED BY THE CRITICS

Thompson formed his first band, Emil & the Detectives, while still in school. By 18, he was playing with the newly formed Fairport Convention. By the time of their first album in 1969, Thompson was already crafting thoughtful songs with unconventional lyrics such as 'Meet On The Ledge', 'Genesis Hall' and 'Crazy Man Michael'. In January 1971, Thompson left to release his first solo album, *Henry The Human Fly* (1972). While recording this he met and later married Linda Peters, who became the primary interpreter of his songs. Their first album, *I Want To See The Bright Lights Tonight* (1974), impressed critics but did not sell well. The Thompsons recorded two more albums before retreating to a commune in East Anglia. They re-emerged in 1977 and two albums, *First Light* (1978) and *Sunnyvista* (1979), built their fan base. Finally, *Shoot Out The Lights* (1982) was lauded by critics, but by this time, the marriage was over.

In 1985 Thompson released *Across A Crowded Room* (1985) and began a long association with American producer Mitchell Froom. In 1990, he recorded his most popular album *Rumor & Sigh*, which earned a Grammy nomination. Thompson has continued to record unique albums, among them *Mirror Blue* (1994), *Mock Tudor* (1999) and *Sweet Warrior* (2007).

**DATE OF BIRTH**

3 April 1949

**PLACE OF BIRTH**

London, England

**GENRES**

Pop

# GLENN TIPTON

## JUDAS PRIEST TO ROCK GOD

Glenn Tipton was a latecomer to the guitar, first picking it up at the age of 21. By the early Seventies, he was making a name for himself on the Birmingham club circuit in the early metal outfit Flying Hat Band. In 1974 guitarist K.K. Downing asked Tipton to join his own burgeoning metal band, Judas Priest. The partnership proved a winning formula and Priest became one of the most influential heavy metal acts of the Seventies.

In those formative years, Tipton maintained a primarily blues-influenced approach to his metal noodlings, occasionally adding brushstrokes of neo-classical phrasing. Sonically, Tipton favoured a Fender Stratocaster, later switching to a modified Strat, swapping its standard single-coil pickup for a fatter-sounding humbucking pickup. As Priest's sound began to modernize, with the mainstream success of *British Steel* (1980), *Point of Entry* (1981) and *Screaming For Vengeance* (1982), so too did Tipton's sound and approach. During the Screaming For Vengeance tour, he switched to the metal-approved Gibson SG, before getting an endorsement deal with Hamer Guitars, which crafted Tipton's signature-model Phantom GT. After a lull through the Nineties, Judas Priest revived their storied career, headlining festival tours and, in the process, exposing a new generation of metalheads to one of the genre's true progenitors. In 2008 they released *Nostradamus*, a concept album based around the sixteenth-century French prophet's work.

**DATE OF BIRTH**

25 October 1947

**PLACE OF BIRTH**

Blackheath, England

**GENRES**

Heavy Metal

# PETER TOSH
## A WAILING WAILER

In the early Sixties Peter Tosh met Bob Marley and Bunny Wailer, and the trio began harmonizing and playing guitars together. In 1962 they formed The Wailing Wailers. The band recorded several successful ska singles before splitting in late 1965. After immersion in the Rastafari movement, the original trio reunited and renamed the group The Wailers. The band left ska behind, and added socially conscious lyrics to their down-tempo grooves. The Wailers teamed with production wizard Lee Perry to record the early reggae hits 'Soul Rebel', 'Duppy Conqueror' and 'Small Axe'. Adding bassist Aston 'Family Man' Barrett and his brother, drummer Carlton, in 1970, The Wailers became Caribbean superstars and signed a recording contract with Island Records. Their debut, *Catch A Fire* (1973), was followed by *Burnin'* the same year.

Tosh's post-Wailers career was characterized by the rebellious title track from his solo debut, *Legalize It* (1976). As Marley became an icon with the positive message of 'One Love', Tosh railed against the establishment. He released *Equal Rights* (1977), *Bush Doctor* (1978), *Mystic Man* (1979) and *Wanted Dread And Alive* (1981). After the release of 1983's *Mama Africa*, Tosh withdrew, returning in 1987 with *No Nuclear War*. He was killed by a gang in 1987.

### DATE OF BIRTH/DEATH
19 October 1944/11 September 1987
### PLACE OF BIRTH
Westmoreland, Jamaica
### GENRES
Regaae, Ska, R&B

# ALI FARKA TOURÉ

## WORLDS APART

Many consider Ali 'Farka' Touré's music to be a bridge between traditional Malian music and its presumed descendant, the blues. He was born in the Muslim village of Kanau on the banks of the Niger River and only occasionally sang in English, usually performing in one of several African languages, mostly Songhay, Fulfulde, Tamasheq or Bambara, as on his breakthrough album, *Ali Farka Touré* (1989), which established his reputation in the world–music community. After its release he toured often in North America and Europe, and recorded frequently.

After retreating to his homeland to tend his farm, he was persuaded to record 1994's *Talking Timbuktu*, a popular collaboration with Ry Cooder. Touré found success taxing and returned home again. Finally, in 1999 Touré released *Niafunké*, an album of more traditional African rhythms. After another hiatus, in 2005 Nonesuch issued *Red & Green*, two albums Touré recorded in the early Eighties, packaged as a two–disc set. Also in 2005, he released the album *In The Heart Of The Moon*, a collaboration with Toumani Diabaté, for which he received a second Grammy Award. Touré's last album, *Savane*, was released posthumously in 2006 and topped the chart for three consecutive months.

**DATE OF BIRTH/DEATH**

31 October 1939/7 March 2006

**PLACE OF BIRTH**

Kanau, Mali

**GENRES**

Traditional African, Blues

A-Z OF
GUITAR GODS

# PETE TOWNSHEND

## THE WHO'S WHO OF ROCK

Pioneering guitarist and The Who's creative force, Pete Townshend began playing banjo in Dixieland outfit the Confederates with school friend John Entwistle. When bassist Entwistle joined The Detours, fronted by Roger Daltrey, Townshend followed. With the recruitment of drummer Keith Moon, the classic Who line-up was complete (though they briefly performed as The High Numbers). The Who's unique sound was unleashed on their 1965 debut single 'I Can't Explain' and their first album, *My Generation* (1965), was a mix of R&B and pop.

After an uncertain year in 1968, the band released *Tommy* (1969), hailed as the first rock opera. *Live at Leeds* (1970) captured the original line-up at its peak. Townshend's blues riffs and solos on Mose Allison's 'Young Man Blues' and his extended soloing on 'My Generation' are driving forces. The Who consolidated their position with the acclaimed *Who's Next* (1971) and a second rock opera, *Quadrophenia* (1973). In between Townshend made his first solo album, *Who Came First* (1972). Shortly after the release of *Who Are You* (1978) Moon died, but the band continued. Townshend pursued a parallel solo career, achieving success with *Empty Glass* (1980). In 1983 he declared that The Who were finished. Since 1996, Townshend has worked with various incarnations of the band. With Daltrey, Townshend made a new Who album, *Endless Wire* (2006).

**DATE OF BIRTH**

19 May 1945

**PLACE OF BIRTH**

London, England

**GENRES**

Rock, Pop, Hard Rock

# IKE TURNER

## THE RHYTHM KING

Rock'n'roll pioneer Ike Turner (pictured left) displayed an early interest in music while working for a local radio station. He formed The Rhythm Kings in the late Forties and, in 1951, they made what many consider to be the first rock'n'roll record, 'Rocket 88'. Produced by Sam Phillips at Sun Studios, the single contained the first recorded example of distorted guitar, caused by Ike's faulty amp. The Rhythm Kings relocated to St Louis where Turner acted as an A&R man for local independent record companies and played guitar with many of his blues heroes. In 1957, during an open mic spot, the teenage Anna Mae Bullock so impressed Turner that he recruited her as a backing singer. Renamed Tina (pictured right), she became lead vocalist and, within a year, Turner's wife. The Rhythm Kings morphed into The Ike & Tina Turner Revue. As simply Ike & Tina Turner, they created an explosive live act that was never adequately captured on vinyl.

After many years of physical and mental abuse, Tina walked out mid–tour in 1976. In 1989, Turner was imprisoned on drugs charges but he returned to recording in 1993, slowly attempting to repair his tarnished reputation. He died of a cocaine overdose in 2007.

### DATE OF BIRTH/DEATH

5 November 1931/12 December 2007

### PLACE OF BIRTH

Clarksdale, USA

### GENRES

Rock'n'Roll, R&B, Funk, Soul Blues

# STEVE VAI

## LEGEND AMONG LEGENDS

Steve Vai began taking guitar lessons from his schoolmate Joe Satriani when he was 14. He later developed an obsession with transcribing Frank Zappa guitar solos. Zappa hired him in 1979, and he appeared on several albums, including *Tinsel Town Rebellion* (1981) and *The Man From Utopia* (1983). He left Zappa in 1982 and recorded his first solo album, *Flex-Able* (1984). That year he joined Alcatrazz, replacing Yngwie Malmsteen. After *Disturbing The Peace* (1985), Vai accepted an offer to join David Lee Roth's post–Van Halen band. *Eat 'Em And Smile* (1986) and *Skyscraper* (1988) combined the band's fire with Roth's showmanship.

Vai left Roth's band in 1989 and temporarily joined Whitesnake before recording a solo album, *Passion And Warfare* (1990), splicing reflective compositions with bursts of intense guitar. He formed a conventional rock band for *Sex & Religion* (1993), but returned to his standard format for *Alien Love Secrets* (1995) and *Fire Garden* (1996). In 1996 he took part in the first G3 tour with Satriani and Eric Johnson and has played on almost every tour since. Vai has continued to release both live and studio albums, the latest of which is the live album and DVD, *Where The Wild Things Are* (2009). Like Satriani, Vai favours Ibanez guitars with a DiMarzio pick-up. In the Nineties he pioneered the use of seven-string guitar.

**DATE OF BIRTH**

6 June 1960

**PLACE OF BIRTH**

North Hempstead, USA

**GENRES**

Hard Rock, Instrumental Rock, Heavy Metal, Progressive Rock

# EDDIE VAN HALEN

## HAIL TO HEAVY METAL

Eddie Van Halen and his brother Alex formed a band in 1972, recruiting bassist Michael Anthony and singer David Lee Roth. The album *Van Halen* (1978) made an immediate impact, with a swaggering rock style vigorously displayed on 'Running With The Devil' and 'You Really Got Me'. *Van Halen II* (1979) capitalized on their success, and *Women And Children First* (1980) and *Fair Warning* (1981) consolidated Van Halen's position. With *Diver Down* (1982) Eddie refined and developed his own style on the instrumentals 'Cathedral' and 'Intruder'. Following Eddie's groundbreaking solo on Michael Jackson's 'Beat It', the album *1984* (1984) produced the No. 1 hit 'Jump'. Growing tension between Eddie and Roth, however, led to the singer's departure in 1985.

Van Halen's success continued with new vocalist Sammy Hagar. The album *5150* (1986) finally gave them a No. 1 and the chemistry between Eddie's riffs and Hagar's vocals was evident on the hits 'Why Can't This Be Love' and 'Love Walks In'. *OU812* (1988) and *For Unlawful Carnal Knowledge* (1991) also hit No. 1. The rapport between Eddie and Hagar was strong on *Balance* (1995). *Van Halen III* (1998) garnered a mixed reaction. In 2007 Van Halen were inducted into the Rock And Roll Hall Of Fame and began an American tour.

**DATE OF BIRTH**

26 January 1955

**PLACE OF BIRTH**

Amsterdam, The Netherlands

**GENRES**

Hard Rock, Heavy Metal

A-Z OF
GUITAR GODS

# STEVIE RAY VAUGHAN

## REVIVING THE BLUES

Exploding on to a generally lethargic blues scene in 1983 with his *Texas Flood* album, Stevie Ray Vaughan administered a high-voltage charge that revitalized the genre with his stunning, ecstatic playing and imagination. He began performing in various bar bands and, in 1975, co-founded Triple Threat with singer Lou Ann Barton. Three years later Vaughan took over vocals and brought in bassist Tommy Shannon to join drummer Chris Layton, renaming the trio Double Trouble. Several successful discs followed, including *Texas Flood* (1983), *Couldn't Stand The Weather* (1984) and *Soul To Soul* (1985).

By this time Vaughan was a global blues star, collaborating with other artists, recording with Albert King on *In Session* (1983), Johnny Copeland on *Texas Twister* (1984) and Lonnie Mack on *Strike Like Lightning* (1985). But his drug abuse caused health problems and, in 1986, he collapsed during a European tour. He resumed touring in 1988. The Grammy Award-winning *In Step* (1989) showed renewed vigour and commitment with Vaughan's impassioned takes on songs such as Buddy Guy's 'Leave My Girl Alone' and Howlin' Wolf's 'Love Me Darlin''. In 1990 Vaughan recorded *Family Style* with his brother Jimmie but, before it was released, he was killed in a helicopter crash returning from a concert in Wisconsin. He was 35 years old.

### DATE OF BIRTH/DEATH

3 October 1954/27 August 1990

### PLACE OF BIRTH

Dallas, USA

### GENRES

Blues, Electric Blues, Blues Rock

A-Z OF
GUITAR GODS

# TOM VERLAINE

## EXPERIMENTER EXTRAORDINAIRE

Tom Verlaine formed the short-lived Neon Boys with kindred spirit Richard Hell while at boarding school. The band became Television a few months later when Verlaine found second guitarist Richard Lloyd, but Hell left to form The Heartbreakers. In 1975, Television began playing legendary New York venues Max's Kansas City and CBGB, where the city's new-wave movement began to ferment. The band released their first single, 'Little Johnny Jewel', independently in 1975. For the recording, Verlaine plugged his guitar straight into the mixing desk. Television's debut album *Marquee Moon* (1977) was hailed as a masterpiece. After a disappointing follow-up, *Adventure* (1978), the band split and Verlaine launched a solo career with *Tom Verlaine* (1979). Later albums showcased his sparkling guitar work, highlighted by a fine solo on 'Ancient Egypt' from *The Wonder* (1990) and the all-instrumental *Warm And Cool* (1992). Television reformed for a third, eponymous album in 1992 and have performed together occasionally since.

Verlaine has consistently sought unconventional guitar sounds. He favours Fender guitars and his use of the company's Jazzmaster and Jaguar models in Television's early days inspired Thurston Moore, Kevin Shields and John Frusciante to do likewise.

### DATE OF BIRTH

13 December 1949

### PLACE OF BIRTH

Morristown, USA

### GENRES

Punk, New Wave

# T-BONE WALKER

## TURNING BLUES ELECTRIC

The first bluesman to record with an electric guitar, T-Bone Walker shaped the course of post-war blues, influencing everyone from B.B. King and Chuck Berry to Jimi Hendrix and beyond. Walker grew up in a musical household in Dallas and by the age of 16 he was playing local shows. In 1929 he won a talent contest to join Cab Calloway's band and made his first recordings. In 1934 he moved to California, where he played and sang in various big bands.

Walker started playing amplified guitar in order to be heard, and his defining moment came in 1942 at a recording session with Freddie Slack's Big Band when he got the chance to take the spotlight for a couple of blues songs. 'Mean Old World' was arguably the first electric blues record. He scored a succession of hits with 'Call It Stormy Monday', 'T-Bone Shuffle' and 'Cold Cold Feeling'. Walker's big-band background and the jazz musicians who played with him gave his blues a sophistication that was in marked contrast to the raw style coming out of Chicago and the rock'n'roll coming out of Memphis. Ironically, this made him unfashionable for a while, although his reputation as a live performer never dipped.

### DATE OF BIRTH/DEATH

26 May 1910/15 March 1975

### PLACE OF BIRTH

Linden, USA

### GENRES

Blues, Electric Blues

# JOE WALSH

## THE OUTRAGEOUS EAGLE

Joe Walsh played bass in various bands before adopting guitar for a stint in the local group The Measles from 1965 to 1969. That led to a spot with Cleveland-based trio The James Gang, with whom Walsh appeared on the band's debut *Yer Album* (1969). The follow-up *James Gang Rides Again* produced the rock-radio staple 'Funk #49' (1970). Walsh then formed the group Barnstorm and hit big with the solo follow-up *The Smoker You Drink, The Player You Get* (1973) and its smash hit 'Rocky Mountain Way'. In the wake of expanding solo success, Walsh adopted an even bigger profile in 1976 as the new guitarist in The Eagles.

While with The Eagles, Walsh continued to release solo material, including *But Seriously Folks* (1978), which included his brilliant comic statement on the rock life, 'Life's Been Good'. In the Eighties Walsh maintained a lower profile, but with The Eagles' reunion in 1994 he returned to the road and the studio for the band's live *Hell Freezes Over* set and *Long Road Out Of Eden* (2007). His outrageous antics and considerable talents have helped Walsh forge one of the best-known and most endearing personalities in rock.

**DATE OF BIRTH**

20 November 1947

**PLACE OF BIRTH**

Wichita, USA

**GENRES**

Rock, Hard Rock, Country Rock, Folk Rock

A-Z OF
GUITAR GODS

# JOHNNY 'GUITAR' WATSON

## HERO OF ALL GENRES

Johnny Watson was a pianist when he arrived in LA at the age of 15, although he was also able to play guitar. It wasn't until he saw Guitar Slim perform that he made it his main instrument. In 1954 Watson recorded the instrumental 'Space Guitar', a riot of reverb and feedback. During the Fifties Watson switched between blues and rock'n'roll, touring with Little Richard, Johnny Otis, Etta James and B.B. King. He had an R&B hit with 'These Lonely Lonely Nights' in 1955 and recorded the first of several versions of his theme tune, 'Gangster Of Love'. He recorded several albums throughout the Sixties, including the misleadingly titled, jazzy *The Blues Soul Of Johnny Guitar Watson* (1964), the live *Larry Williams Show With Johnny Guitar Watson* (1965) and the soulful *Two For The Price Of One* (1967).

In the early Seventies he took his soul in a funkier direction with *Listen* (1973) and *I Don't Want To Be Alone, Stranger* (1975) before finding a flashy disco connection with the highly successful *Ain't That A Bitch* (1976) and *Giant* (1978), among others. He returned with the funk/rap *Bow Wow* in 1994. He was making a live comeback when he suffered a fatal heart attack in 1996.

### DATE OF BIRTH/DEATH

3 February 1935/17 May 1996

### PLACE OF BIRTH

Houston, USA

### GENRES

Blues, Electric Blues, Blues Rock, Disco, FunkRap

# PAUL WELLER

## THE MODFATHER

Paul Weller was a boyhood Beatles fanatic before discovering The Who and, through them, the mod movement. The Jam was formed at secondary school, and Weller originally played bass. The band's arrival in London coincided with the burgeoning punk scene, and seeing the Sex Pistols live was a pivotal moment for Weller. While adopting punk's energy, The Jam remained distinct from the movement, not least because of the band's musical ability. Their best album, *All Mod Cons* (1978), showcases Weller's maturing style and use of techniques ranging from power chords ('Billy Hunt') to acoustic-electric work ('Fly') and backwards masking ('In The Crowd'). At the height of The Jam's popularity in 1982, Weller disbanded the outfit, citing frustration with the limitations of the three-piece format.

His next project, The Style Council, a loose confederation of musicians, enabled him to explore more diverse musical areas, adding Latin and jazz to his repertoire. The Style Council folded in 1989, leaving Weller out of favour and without a recording contract. Influenced by the classic rock of Traffic, Free and Neil Young, Weller returned to basics by playing live and mounted an impressive comeback, beginning with his self-titled solo debut in 1992 and culminating in the million-selling *Stanley Road* (1995). A late-period purple patch has also seen Weller release the acclaimed *22 Dreams* (2005) and *Wake Up The Nation* (2010).

### DATE OF BIRTH

25 May 1958

### PLACE OF BIRTH

Woking, England

### GENRES

Rock, Mod, Soul, Latin, Jazz

A-Z OF
GUITAR GODS

# CLARENCE WHITE

## INNOVATOR OF COUNTRY ROCK

Born into a family of musicians, White played with his brothers in The Country Boys, which became The Kentucky Colonels. His skills led to session work on many mid–Sixties pop and rock albums, as well as live gigs alongside Gene Parsons, Gib Gilbeau and former Byrd Gene Clark. White (pictured left, beside Roger McGuinn) joined Parsons and Gilbeau in the band Nashville West and was invited to record with The Byrds. White's innovative string bending and solos on the group's seminal *Sweetheart Of The Rodeo* (1968) album enlivened tracks such as 'The Christian Life' and 'One Hundred Years From Now'. In 1968 he joined the band and toured with them until their final split in 1973.

With fellow Byrd Gene Parsons White developed a device, the B–Bender, that would allow guitarists to bend strings independently of their fretting hands, giving six–string guitarists the mournful sound of a pedal steel with less work. The sound is perhaps most familiar from Bernie Leadon's solo on The Eagle's 'Peaceful Easy Feeling' (1972), but has been used on records by artists as diverse as Led Zeppelin and Donna Summer. White, however, didn't live to see his invention gain its following. He was killed by a drunk driver after a performance with The Kentucky Colonels in 1973.

## DATE OF BIRTH/DEATH

7 June 1944/15 July 1973

## PLACE OF BIRTH

Lewiston, USA

## GENRES

Country Rock, Rock, Bluegrass

# JACK WHITE

## REVIVING THE BLUES

Jack White was born John Gillis in Detroit, Michigan. He taught himself to play drums and on leaving school played in various Detroit bands. In 1996, he married Meg White and, reversing normal practice, took her surname. The White Stripes were born when Meg, with no previous experience, started bashing along to his guitar. After two independent albums, their breakthrough came with *White Blood Cells* (2001). White was hailed as the most explosive rock performer in the world and credited with returning the blues to the forefront of modern rock.

The White Stripes' success initiated a new era of back-to-basics rock. White's most famous guitar is a red and white Airline, a cheap Sixties department-store model. For the White Stripes he also uses a Harmony Rocket, a Crestwood Astral and a Gretsch White Penguin. In his band The Raconteurs he favours Gretsch guitars. To achieve a powerful live sound, he makes extensive use of effects, mainly a DigiTech Whammy to shift the pitch down and compensate for the absence of bass. When playing barre and power chords, he uses the little finger on his left hand partly because of an injury to his index finger sustained in a car accident in 2003. White has since made his name as producer and label svengali, launching his Third Man imprint and continuing to found new projects, most notably The Dead Weather, with The Kills' Alison Mosshart and members of The Raconteurs. *Sea of Cowards*, the follow-up to 2009's *Horehound*, was released in 2010.

### DATE OF BIRTH

9 July 1975

### PLACE OF BIRTH

Detroit, USA

### GENRES

Punk Blues, Alternative Rock, Pop Rock

A-Z OF
GUITAR GODS

# JOHN WILLIAMS

## THE SKY'S THE LIMIT

Classical guitarist–composer John Williams has explored many styles beyond his traditional classical training. At the age of 12 he went to Italy to study under Andrés Segovia and later studied piano at the Royal College of Music. He was a member of the fusion group Sky and is also a composer and arranger. He enjoyed a worldwide hit single with his recording of 'Cavatina' by Stanley Myers. In 1973, Cleo Laine wrote lyrics and recorded the song 'He Was Beautiful', accompanied by Williams. A year later, it was a Top 5 UK hit single for Iris Williams (no relation). Williams created a highly acclaimed classical–rock fusion duet with Pete Townshend of The Who for Townshend's 'Won't Get Fooled Again' and his classical–rock fusion band Sky gave the first rock concert at Westminster Abbey.

Williams has appeared on over 100 albums (including compilations). He was a professor of guitar at the Royal College of Music in London from 1960 to 1973. Besides film soundtracks, Williams has rearranged Beatles songs, played electric guitar and formed his own ensembles (John Williams & Friends, Attacca) to explore other music. On the album release *The Guitarist* (1998) he used Turkish and Greek rhythms and harmonies to support medieval music. *The Magic Box* (2002) examines African music. In 2007 he received the Edison lifetime achievement award.

**DATE OF BIRTH**

24 April 1941

**PLACE OF BIRTH**

Melbourne, Australia

**GENRES**

Classical, Classical–Rock Fusion, African

A-Z OF GUITAR GODS

# JOHNNY WINTER

## BLUES DEVOTION

Cross–eyed and albino from birth, Johnny Winter showed a precocious talent for music, taking up clarinet at the age of five and switching to guitar after a brief flirtation with the ukulele. He formed his first group, Johnny & the Jammers, with brother Edgar. Winter went on to play in several blues bands during the mid– to late Sixties. His break came in 1969 when an album he had recorded as part of a trio came to the attention of two *Rolling Stone* journalists, leading to its release as *Johnny Winter* (1969) on CBS.

Hailed as the new superstar blues guitarist, his fourth album, *Johnny Winter And* (1970), confirmed his success and featured the song that became his signature tune, Rick Derringer's 'Rock'n'Roll Hoochie Koo'. Derringer was added to the band on second guitar on *Live Johnny Winter And* (1971). Suffering from drug addiction and depression, Winter took a break, returning for *Still Alive And Well* (1973). He produced two albums for Muddy Waters, *Hard Again* (1977) and Waters' final work *King Bee* (1980). His own *Nothing But The Blues* (1977) was made with members of Muddy's touring band. Still touring despite health problems, Winter eschews his rock hits to concentrate on the blues.

**DATE OF BIRTH**

23 February 1944

**PLACE OF BIRTH**

Beaumont, USA

**GENRES**

Blues Rock, Electric Blues, Rock'n'Roll

# ZAKK WYLDE

## THE LAST TRUE HERO

Wylde started playing guitar at the age of 15, drawing influence from such legends as Jimmy Page, Eddie Van Halen and Randy Rhoads. He started a band called Stone Henge, playing *Animal House*-style house parties in central New Jersey. A few years later a photographer offered to get his press kit into the hands of Ozzy Osbourne, who was looking for a new guitarist. A short while later, Wylde was making his debut with the Prince of Darkness at Wormwood Scrubs prison, in London, England. From the start, Wylde's minor pentatonic-based lines, aggressive vibrato and screaming pinch harmonics proved a perfect fit for the Osbourne sound. *No More Tears* (1991) solidified Wylde's reputation as a guitarist here to stay. Indeed, since that time, Wylde has recorded three more studio records with him, including 2007's *Black Rain*.

In addition to his Ozzy gig, Wylde has worked on several side projects, such as *Pride And Glory* (1994) and a solo album titled *Book Of Shadows* (1996). But Wylde's most prolific work has been with his own Black Label Society. Since 1999, BLS has released seven studio records and several live albums and DVDs. Additionally, Wylde has several signature-model Gibson Les Paul Customs and a signature-model Marshall head.

### DATE OF BIRTH

14 February 1967

### PLACE OF BIRTH

Bayonne, USA

### GENRES

Heavy Metal, Hard Rock, Southern Rock

# ANGUS YOUNG

## ON A HIGHWAY TO HERO

AC/DC guitarist Angus Young is larger than life – all five feet two inches of him. Rising up from working-class Scottish roots to become the heart and soul of one of the greatest rock'n'roll bands of all time, Young, with his schoolboy outfit and Gibson SG in hand, has become the definitive rock-guitar icon. He teamed up with brother Malcolm to form AC/DC in 1973. After a couple of years, they hooked up with singer Bon Scott and signed a deal with Atlantic Records, releasing their debut, *High Voltage*, in 1975. Contrary to the glam-rock and disco popular in the mid-Seventies, AC/DC pounded out no-nonsense three-chord rock with a good-time message. Although there were countless rock guitarists playing power chords and minor pentatonic licks on Gibson SGs through Marshall amps, *nobody* sounded like Angus Young.

After several more successful albums, including 1979's *Highway to Hell*, tragedy struck, when singer Scott died of acute alcohol poisoning. Downhearted, the band nearly called it quits, until they met British singer Brian Johnson. The fit was perfect and AC/DC rebounded with one of the top five albums in rock history, *Back In Black* (1980), which enshrined AC/DC as the world's greatest rock'n'roll band. Millions of albums later, AC/DC have retained their iconic status, releasing the chart-topping *Black Ice* in 2008 and recording the soundtrack to *Iron Man 2* in 2010.

**DATE OF BIRTH**

31 March 1955

**PLACE OF BIRTH**

Glasgow, Scotland

**GENRES**

Heavy Metal, Hard Rock, Rock'n'Roll

# MALCOLM YOUNG

## POWER BEHIND THE THRONE

Malcolm founded AC/DC with brother Angus in 1973 and the recruitment of vocalist Bon Scott the following year provided the catalyst for the band's unstoppable rise from their early Australian-only albums to international stardom with *Highway To Hell* (1979). AC/DC survived Scott's death, bouncing back to even greater success with new frontman Brian Johnson. Although less visible than the ostentatious Angus, Malcolm Young is the power behind the throne of AC/DC: he is chief decision-maker and co-songwriter. Providing the foundation for his younger brother's guitar heroics, Malcolm nails down the rhythm on his 1963 Gretsch Jet Firebird, although for the tours in support of *Back In Black* (1980) and *For Those About To Rock (We Salute You)* (1981), he played a Gretsch White Falcon.

His style is simple, direct and brutal; he plugs straight into the amps and shuns the use of effects. AC/DC standards such as 'Highway To Hell' and 'Problem Child' are built on his insistent three-chord riffs. AC/DC's guitar sound influenced the New Wave of British Heavy Metal which arose in the late Seventies; bands such as Saxon and Iron Maiden have acknowledged their debt to the expatriate Scots, whilst Malcolm Young's riffs have inspired speed metal, thrash and grunge.

**DATE OF BIRTH**

6 January 1953

**PLACE OF BIRTH**

Glasgow, Scotland

**GENRES**

Heavy Metal, Hard Rock, Rock'n'Roll

A-Z OF GUITAR GODS

# NEIL YOUNG

## UNIVERSAL APPEAL

Neil Young dropped out of high school to form Neil Young & the Squires, and later played the Toronto coffeehouse circuit, where he met a number of folk artists, including guitarists Richie Furay and Stephen Stills, with whom he formed Buffalo Springfield. They hit big with Stills' counterculture anthem 'For What It's Worth' and recorded three albums before splintering in 1968. Young signed a solo deal with Reprise Records, and his second solo effort, *Everybody Knows This Is Nowhere* (1969), with his new backing band Crazy Horse, became a major hit. Young joined David Crosby, Steven Stills and Graham Nash's supergroup in the summer of 1969. Young eventually recorded five albums (including two live albums) as part of Crosby, Stills & Nash, contributing the hits 'Helpless' and 'Ohio'. His solo career simultaneously blossomed. *Harvest* was the biggest-selling album of 1972, and 'Heart Of Gold' remains Young's most successful single.

Young was hailed by punk rockers, grunge artists and country fans alike because of albums such as *Rust Never Sleeps* (1979), *Freedom* (1989), *Broken Arrow* (1996) and *Harvest Moon* (1992). He continues to release a new album nearly every year, including 2009's *Fork In The Road*, while simultaneously releasing rare live recordings and a remastered back catalogue working with his *Archives* project. Young collected guitars, but onstage and in the studio he used just a few instruments, including a 1953 Gibson Les Paul Goldtop and a Martin D-45.

**DATE OF BIRTH**

12 November 1945

**PLACE OF BIRTH**

Toronto, Canada

**GENRES**

Rock

# FRANK ZAPPA

## FATHER OF HARMONY

Born in 1940, Zappa grew up in Los Angeles and wrote film scores in the early Sixties before forming the Mothers Of Invention in 1965. His guitar playing on *Freak Out!* (1966), *Absolutely Free* (1967) and *We're Only In It For The Money* (1968) was succinct, but he began stretching out on solo albums such as *Hot Rats* (1969), *Apostrophe (')* (1974), *One Size Fits All* (1975) and *Zoot Allures* (1978). Zappa's reputation was enhanced by extended guitar solos on a succession of live albums through the Seventies – *Live At The Fillmore East* (1971), *Roxy & Elsewhere* (1974), *Live In New York* (1977) and *Sheik Yerbouti* (1979).

In 1979 Zappa continued to push his own boundaries with the rock musical *Joe's Garage*, composed of *Acts I, II & III*, and in 1981 he encouraged his guitar fan club with a triple album set called *Shut Up 'N Play Yer Guitar* that featured 'solos and nothing else'. *Ship Arriving Too Late To Save A Drowning Witch* (1982) – featuring 'Valley Girl', the closest he came to a hit single – and *Jazz From Hell* (1987), which won a Grammy for Best Rock Instrumental Performance. By the time of his death from prostate cancer in 1993, Zappa had amassed a catalogue of more than 60 albums.

**DATE OF BIRTH/DEATH**

21 December 1940/4 December 1993

**PLACE OF BIRTH**

Los Angeles, USA

**GENRES**

Rock, Jazz, Classical

# ACKNOWLEDGEMENTS

## AUTHOR BIOGRAPHIES

### MICK TAYLOR (Foreword)

Mick Taylor started 'playing' the guitar at a tender two years old, bashing his gut-string toy instrument to pieces until his parents realized the bashing would stop when they tuned it to a chord. At eight years old he received his first electric guitar and by 13 he was playing in bars, pubs and events near his home. A keen writer, Mick sought to combine his passions and headed straight for *Guitarist* magazine after university as a junior. Mick has also worked on *Metal Hammer, Mountain Biking UK* and *Guitar Buyer* magazines before returning to his dream job as editor of *Guitarist* in February 2007.

### RUSTY CUTCHIN (Consultant Editor and Author)

Rusty Cutchin has been a musician, recording engineer, producer and journalist for over 25 years. He has been technical editor and a columnist for *Guitar One* magazine as well as an associate editor of *Electronic Musician* magazine and editor in chief of *Home Recording* magazine. Prior to that he was a recording engineer with credits on albums by Mariah Carey, Richie Sambora, Yoko Ono and many others. Cutchin has been a consultant editor and contributor to nine books on subjects such as the guitar, computer recording technology and rock history, including *The Illustrated Encyclopedia of Guitar Heroes, The Illustrated Home Recording Handbook* and *The Definitive Guitar Handbook*.

### HUGH FIELDER (Author)

Hugh Fielder can remember the 1960s even though he was there. He can remember the 1970s and 1980s because he was at *Sounds* magazine (RIP) and the 1990s because he was editor of Tower Records' *TOP* magazine. He has shared a spliff with Bob Marley, a glass of wine with David Gilmour, a pint with Robert Plant, a cup of tea with Keith Richards and a frosty stare with Axl Rose. He has watched Mike Oldfield strip naked in front of him and Bobby Womack fall asleep while he was interviewing him.

### MIKE GENT (Author)

Nurturing an obsession with pop music which dates back to first hearing Slade's 'Gudbuy T'Jane' in 1972, Mike Gent remains fixated, despite failing to master any musical instrument, with the possible exception of the recorder. A freelance writer since 2001, he has contributed to *Writers' Forum, Book and Magazine Collector, Record Buyer, When Saturday Comes, Inside David Bowie and the Spiders* (DVD), *The Kinks 1964–1978* (DVD), *The Beatles 1962–1970* (DVD), *Remember the Eighties, Where Were You When? – Music That Changed Our Lives, The Definitive Illustrated Encyclopedia of Rock* and *The Little Book of the World Cup*. His personal guitar god is Johnny Marr.

**MICHAEL MUELLER (Author)**

Michael Mueller is a New York–based guitarist, author, editor and journalist. He is the former editor–in–chief of *Guitar One* magazine, where he interviewed such legendary guitarists as Angus Young, Joe Satriani, John Petrucci, Steve Vai, Zakk Wylde, Eric Johnson, Mark Tremonti and Frank Gambale, among many others. Currently, he is a contributor to *Guitar Edge* magazine and *GuitarInstructor.com*. He has also written for *Guitar World, Women Who Rock* and *Home Recording*. As an author, Mueller has written several instructional books, including the *Hal Leonard Rock Guitar Method, Jazz For the Rock Guitarist* (Hal Leonard) and *Sight Reading for the Rock Guitarist* (Cherry Lane). Additionally, he has worked behind the scenes to produce several instructional guitar videos for the Hal Leonard Corporation, including the *Hal Leonard Guitar Method, Best of Lennon & McCartney* (for electric, acoustic, and bass guitar) and *Guitar Soloing*.

**DAVE SIMONS (Author)**

Dave Simons is a musician and journalist, and has covered the recording arts, past and present, for a variety of publications including *Home Recording, Guitar One* and *Musician*. His recent books include *Studio Stories: How the Great New York Records Were Made* (Backbeat) and *Read the Beatles: Classic and New Writings on the Beatles, Their Legacy, and Why They Still Matter* (Penguin).

# PiCTURE CREDiTS

# RESOURCES

## FURTHER READING

Assante, E., *Legends of Rock: The Artists, Instruments, Myths and History of 50 Years of Youth Music*, White Star, 2007

Bockris, V., *Keith Richards: The Biography*, De Capo Press, 2003

Carcieri, M., *Prince: A Life in Music*, iUniverse Inc., 2004

Carson, A. and Beck, J., *Jeff Beck: Crazy Fingers*, Backbeat Books, 2001

Case, G., *Jimmy Page: Magus, Musician, Man: An Unauthorized Biography*, Hal Leonard, 2007

Chapman, C., *Interviews with the Jazz Greats*, Mel Bay Publications, 2001

Chapman, R. and Clapton, E., *Guitar: Music, History, Players*, DK Publishing, 2003

Charlesworth, C., *A–Z of Rock Guitarists*, Proteus Publishing, 1983

Cherry Lane Music (ed.), *Guitar One Presents Legends of the Lead Guitar: The Best of Interviews: 1995–2000*, Cherry Lane Music, 2001

Christie, I., *Everybody Wants Some: The Van Halen Saga*, Wiley John & Sons, 2007

Clapton, E., *Clapton: The Autobiography*, Broadway Books, 2007

Clayson, A., *Legendary Sessions: The Rolling Stones, Beggars Banquet*, Flame Tree Publishing, 2008

Crawford, B. and Patoski, J., *Stevie Ray Vaughan: Caught in the Crossfire*, Little Brown & Company, 1994

Cross, C., *Room Full of Mirrors: A Biography of Jimi Hendrix*, Hyperion, 2005

Cutchin, R. (ed.), *The Definitive Guitar Handbook*, Flame Tree Publishing, 2008

Dome, M. and Fogg, R., *Eddie Van Halen: Know the Man, Play the Music*, Backbeat Books, 2005

Frame, P., *The Complete Rock Family Trees*, Omnibus Press, 1983

Freeth, N. and Douse, C., *Icons of Music: Great Guitarists*, Thunder Bay Press, 2002

Gill, C., *Guitar Legends: The Definitive Guide to the World's Greatest Guitar Players*, HarperCollins, 1995

Goins, W.E. and McKinney C.R., *A Biography of Charlie Christian, Jazz Guitar's King of Swing*, Edwin Mellen Press, 2005

Gregory, H., *1000 Great Guitarists*, Backbeat Books, 2002

Grouse, L., *Fancy Fretwork: The Great Jazz Guitarists*, Franklin Watts, 2000

Hal Leonard (ed.), *Guitar World Presents the 100 Greatest Guitarists of All Time*, Hal Leonard, 2002

Heatley, M. (ed.), *The Definitive Illustrated Encyclopaedia of Rock*, Flame Tree Publishing, 2006

Jackson, L., *Brian May*, Portrait, 2007

Kempster, G., *Guitars: Sounds, Chrome and Stars*, Flame Tree Publishing, 2007

Kienzle, R., *Great Guitarists: The Most Influential Players in Jazz, Country, Blues and Rock*, Facts on File, 1985

Mairants, I., *The Great Jazz Guitarists: Birth of Bebop Part 1*, Sanctuary Publishing, 2002

Mairants, I., *The Great Jazz Guitarists: On From the 1950s Part 2*, Sanctuary Publishing, 2002

Mason, N., *Inside Out: A Personal History of Pink Floyd*, Chronicle Books, 2005

Newquist, H.P. and Prown, P., *Legends of Rock Guitar*, Hal Leonard, 1997

Obrecht, J., *Rollin' and Tumblin': The Postwar Blues Guitarists*, Backbeat Books, 2000

Ophee, M. (ed.), *Dictionary of Guitarists: A Biographical, Bibliographical, Historical, Critical Dictionary of Guitars, Guitarists, Guitar-Makers, Dances and Songs*, Editions Orphee, 1986

Rolf, J. (ed.), *The Definitive Illustrated Encyclopedia of Jazz and Blues*, Flame Tree Publishing, 2007

Rubin, D., *Birth of the Groove: R&B, Soul and Funk Guitar 1945–1965*, Hal Leonard, 2004

Rubin, D., *Inside the Blues, 1942–1982: Four Decades of the Greatest Electric Blues Guitarists*, Hal Leonard, 2007

Shirley, I., *Led Zeppelin Revealed*, Flame Tree Publishing, 2008

Summers, A. and the Edge, *One Train Later: A Memoir*, St Martin's Press, 2006

Tosone, J., *Classical Guitarists: Conversations*, McFarland & Co., 2000

Whittaker, S.C., *Unsung Heroes of Rock Guitar: 15 Great Rock Guitarists in Their Own Words*, BookSurge Publishing, 2003

Wilkerson, M., *Who Are You: The Life of Pete Townshend*, Omnibus Press, 2008

Woog, A., *Carlos Santana: Legendary Guitarist*, Gale Group, 2006

# WEBSITES

www.artistdirect.com
www.billboard.com
www.classicalguitarist.co.uk
www.classicjazzguitar.com
www.guitaredgemag.com

www.guitarists.net
www.guitarplayer.com
www.guitarworld.com
www.hotguitarist.com
www.kerrang.com

www.modernguitarist.com
www.mojo4music.com
www.musicfirebox.com
www.myspace.com
www.nme.com

www.rockhall.com
www.rollingstone.com
www.ultimaterockgods.com
www.vh1.com
www.worldsgreatestguitarist.com

# INDEX

Page references in *italics* refer to illustrations, and page references in **bold** refer to main articles.